Puglia Travel Guide 2025

2025

Whitewashed Villages With Maps & Images,Cliffs of Polignano a Mare,Cobblestone Streets of Alberobello,Lecce's Baroque,Region's Countless Caves,,Festivals and Events

CAROLE J. HARVEY

Disclaimer

The information provided in this book is for general informational purposes only. While every effort has been made to ensure the accuracy and completeness of the information contained herein, the author and publisher assume no responsibility for any errors, omissions, or changes to travel details, prices, or locations. Readers are encouraged to verify any information with local authorities or service providers before making travel decisions. The author and publisher disclaim any liability for any personal, financial, or travel-related losses or damages incurred through the use of this guide.

Trademark

All product names, logos, and brands mentioned in this book are property of their respective trademark owners. Any use of trademarks or brand names is for descriptive purposes only and does not imply sponsorship, endorsement, or affiliation by or with the trademark holder.

Table Of Content

SCAN THE QR CODE

1. Open your device's camera app.
2. Align the QR code within the camera frame.
3. Wait for the code to be recognized.
4. Check the displayed notification or link.
5. Tap to access the linked content or information.

Chapter 1. Introduction

Welcome to Puglia: A Land of Sun, Sea, and Stories

Welcome to Puglia, the heel of Italy's boot and a treasure trove of timeless charm. I want to begin by thanking you sincerely for choosing this guide. With so many books and resources available, I'm humbled that you've placed your trust in mine. This book isn't just a collection of facts and tips—it's a labor of love, inspired by personal experiences, countless discoveries, and a profound admiration for Puglia's unmatched beauty.

The first time I set foot in Puglia, I felt like I had stumbled upon a secret that the world had yet to fully uncover. As the plane descended, the patchwork of olive groves, whitewashed villages, and shimmering coastline stretched out before me. It was love at first sight.

On my first morning, I found myself wandering the cobblestone streets of Alberobello, mesmerized by the trulli. These charming, cone-roofed houses, seemingly plucked from a storybook, told a tale of ancient ingenuity and resilience. As I sipped an espresso under the shade of an olive tree, the world seemed to slow down, and I realized that Puglia wasn't just a place—it was an experience, a rhythm of life that invites you to pause, breathe, and savor the moment.

Each corner of Puglia holds a special memory for me. The cliffs of Polignano a Mare, where the turquoise waters seem to merge with the sky, left me awestruck. The golden glow of Lecce's Baroque architecture at sunset stirred my soul. The labyrinthine alleys of Ostuni, the "White City," felt like a portal to another time. And then there's the food—the kind of food that makes you close your eyes and smile after every bite. From handmade orecchiette to creamy burrata, every dish tells a story of tradition and passion.

Puglia isn't just a destination; it's an invitation to immerse yourself in its vibrant culture, connect with its warm-hearted people, and lose yourself in its stunning landscapes. This book is your key to unlocking the magic of Puglia. Inside, you'll find detailed insights into its must-visit locations, hidden gems, and practical tips to help you make the most of your adventure.

As you turn these pages, my hope is that you'll feel the same sense of wonder and connection that I experienced. Whether you're here to explore ancient castles, bask in the sun on pristine beaches, or indulge in the region's culinary delights, Puglia has something to offer every traveler.

Thank you once again for allowing me to be a part of your journey. Together, let's discover why Puglia is a place that stays with you long after you've left its shores.

Welcome to Puglia, where every corner has a story and every moment is worth savoring.

How does this feel? Would you like any additional tweaks or personal touches?

The History of Puglia: A Crossroads of Civilizations

Puglia, with its sun-soaked landscapes and ancient olive trees, is a land where history whispers from every stone, every street, and every shoreline. Positioned at the heel of Italy's boot, this region has long been a gateway to the Mediterranean—a crossroads of cultures, empires, and ideas that have shaped its identity over millennia.

The story of Puglia begins in prehistory, as evidenced by the region's countless caves and dolmens. The Grotte di Castellana, a labyrinth of underground caves, reveals traces of early human habitation, suggesting that Puglia has been a sanctuary for life since the Paleolithic era. These early inhabitants left their mark with enigmatic carvings and tools, hints of a world long gone but not forgotten.

As the centuries unfolded, Puglia became a melting pot of civilizations. The Messapians, an ancient Italic tribe, were among the first to settle here, establishing thriving communities and intricate networks of trade. Their influence can still be seen in the remains of fortified walls and settlements scattered across the region.

With its strategic location bridging East and West, Puglia soon attracted the attention of the Greeks. During the 8th century BCE, they established colonies along the coastline, leaving behind a legacy of art, philosophy, and architecture. Taranto, one of Puglia's oldest cities, became a flourishing Greek polis, a hub of culture and commerce that still echoes in the city's ruins and museums today.

The Roman era brought Puglia into the heart of one of history's greatest empires. The Via Appia, the ancient Roman road often called the "Queen of Roads," connected Puglia to the rest of Italy, cementing its role as a vital trade route. Towns like Brindisi and Bari flourished as bustling ports, gateways to the Adriatic and beyond. Roman amphitheaters and aqueducts, many of which still stand, serve as enduring testaments to this era of grandeur.

After the fall of Rome, Puglia became a prize in the power struggles of medieval Europe. The Byzantines, Lombards, and Saracens vied for control, each leaving their imprint on the region. The arrival of the Normans in the 11th century marked a turning point. Under their rule, Puglia experienced a renaissance of art and architecture. The stunning Romanesque cathedrals of Bari, Trani, and Bitonto, with their intricate carvings and imposing facades, stand as monuments to this golden age.

One of the most enigmatic figures in Puglia's history is Emperor Frederick II, often called the "Stupor Mundi" or "Wonder of the World." A lover of science, art, and culture, Frederick made Puglia his stronghold in the 13th century. He constructed the iconic Castel del Monte, a mysterious octagonal fortress that continues to intrigue historians and visitors alike with its perfect geometry and astronomical alignments.

As the Middle Ages gave way to the Renaissance, Puglia's fortunes waxed and waned under various rulers, including the Spanish and the Bourbons. Each era added new layers to its cultural tapestry. By the 19th century, Puglia played a pivotal role in Italy's unification, with its people joining the fight for independence and freedom.

Today, Puglia's history is not confined to museums and monuments. It lives on in the traditions, festivals, and daily lives of its people. The olive groves that stretch endlessly across the landscape are descendants of trees planted centuries ago. The trulli of Alberobello, with their unique conical roofs, are reminders of ancient building techniques passed down through generations.

Walking through Puglia is like stepping into a living history book. Each town, each village, tells a chapter of a story that spans thousands of years. From the whispers of ancient civilizations to the echoes of empires, Puglia's history is a testament to resilience, adaptation, and the enduring spirit of its people.

Why Visit Puglia?

Puglia, located in the heel of Italy's "boot," seems tailor-made for vacationers looking for an original and unique experience. Its sun-soaked beaches and quaint whitewashed villages, as well as its world-renowned food and deep-rooted traditions, fascinate every visitor with its distinct combination of history, culture, and natural beauty. Let me explain why I feel Puglia should be on everyone's trip radar.

A Journey to Timeless Charm

● Puglia is a magical place where time seems to slow down and each corner tells a tale.

● The small cobblestone alleyways of Alberobello, with its comical trulli cottages, and the baroque beauty of Lecce take you back in time.

● These locations showcase exceptional workmanship and attention.

Stunning coastlines and natural beauty

● Puglia is a beach lover's heaven, with immaculate beaches, spectacular cliffs, and clear seas.

● Polignano a Mare, set on limestone cliffs, is picture-perfect, and Salento's beaches match those of the Caribbean with crystal-clear seas.

● Inland, the terrain changes to rolling olive fields, historic wineries, and rocky nature reserves like as Gargano National Park.

Food that touches the soul

● Puglia's food is known for its simplicity, freshness, and deliciousness.

● Culinary highlights include orecchiette pasta, fresh burrata cheese, and focaccia Barese.

● Each meal celebrates local traditions and richness, complemented by strong Primitivo wine.

Warmth of People

● Puglians welcome tourists with warmth and genuine hospitality, making them feel like valued guests.

● From chefs sharing family recipes to merchants providing local suggestions, every connection is memorable.

A Slowly Paced Escape

● Puglia has a slower pace of life, with siestas in the afternoon and leisurely dinners in the evening.

● It's ideal for taking a break and enjoying the present moment without stress.

An Underrated Treasure.

● Puglia is less popular with tourists compared to other areas in Italy.

● Enjoy pristine beauty and genuine experiences without the masses.

Rich History and Culture

Puglia's architecture, art, and customs reflect its past as a crossroads of cultures throughout millennia.

● The region's rich cultural heritage is evident in its ancient ruins, castles, and colourful festivals.

A Destination for All Travelers

Puglia offers a diverse range of activities, including history, gastronomy, wildlife, and beaches.

● Its attractiveness attracts families, couples, and lone tourists alike.

A personal reflection.

For me, Puglia exemplifies what makes travel magical: the opportunity to immerse oneself in beauty, connect with people and places, and return with wonderful experiences. It's more than simply a place; it's an experience—a feeling of excitement, wonder, and belonging that lingers long after you leave.

In Puglia, you don't just see, but you feel. That's what makes it so unique.

Quick facts about the region.

Quick facts about the region.

● Puglia (Apulia in Italian) is situated in southern Italy, making up the "heel" of the country's boot-shaped peninsula. It is surrounded by the Adriatic Sea to the east, the Ionian Sea to the southeast, and the regions of Molise, Campania, and Basilicata to the north and west.

● Bari is the region's capital, a dynamic port city with a rich cultural scene and a beautiful old town.

● Locals speak regional dialects in addition to the national language, Italian. Learning a few simple Italian words will improve your vacation experience.

● Puglia has a population of around 4 million people, dispersed throughout attractive towns, dynamic cities, and stunning rural landscapes.

● Puglia has a Mediterranean climate, with hot, dry summers and warm, wet winters. The location is ideal for summer beach holidays and off-season cultural excursions.

● The region's economy relies heavily on agriculture, namely olive oil, wine, and durum wheat production. Tourism is also becoming a significant contribution to the economy.

● Puglia is known for its "cucina povera," or peasant cookery that uses fresh, locally produced ingredients. Signature meals include orecchiette pasta, burrata cheese, and focaccia Barese.

Puglia has almost 500 miles of coastline with spectacular beaches in Salento, Gargano, and Polignano a Mare, making it one of Italy's most beautiful destinations.

Puglia's historic icons, including Alberobello's trulli dwellings and the 13th-century Castel del Monte, are designated as UNESCO sites.

● Transportation: The area is easily accessible by Bari and Brindisi airports, rail networks, and attractive driving routes. Many places are well-located for day getaways.

Puglia celebrates several festivals throughout the year, including those honouring saints, traditional music, and cuisine.

Chapter 2: Top Attractions

Historic sites.

Alberobello Trulli Houses (UNESCO World Heritage Site)

What to Explore:

● Conical, whitewashed stone Trulli buildings from the 14th century provide unique architecture. They are excellent examples of traditional Apulian drystone construction.

● Visit the Rione Monti District, home to over 1,000 Trulli homes transformed into tourist stores, cafés, and boutique hotels. Highlights include Trullo Sovrano, the biggest and most well-known Trullo, which is now a museum.

● Cultural Significance: Understand the historical and cultural significance of these constructions, which were designed to be readily demolished and escape taxes.

● Visit the Belvedere Santa Lucia lookout for sweeping views of the Trulli-lined streets.

How to get there:

Alberobello is located around 1 hour from Bari and 1.5 hours from Brindisi. Parking is provided near the historic centre.

● Train: Take the Ferrovie Sud Est from Bari or Lecce. The rail station is a 10-minute walk from the Trulli neighbourhood.

● Regional buses link Alberobello to important cities in Puglia, such as Bari and Lecce.

● Air: The nearest airports are Bari and Brindisi. From there, you may hire a vehicle or utilize public transportation.

Cost:

● Free access to the Trulli district. Entry fees for specialized attractions like Trullo Sovrano are typically €2–€5.

Castle del Monte (UNESCO World Heritage Site)

What to Explore:

● Unique Medieval Castle: Emperor Frederick II erected the octagonal Castel del Monte in the 13th century. Its geometric design and astronomical alignments make it a masterpiece of medieval construction.

● Explore the castle's interior, with stone stairs, arched windows, and historical displays. The lofty elevation offers expansive views of the surrounding landscape.

● Historical Significance: The castle's function is unknown, making it an intriguing place to explore. It is believed to have operated as a hunting lodge, garrison, or perhaps an astronomical observatory.

How to get there:

Castel del Monte is a 1-hour trip from Bari and is located near Andria. Parking is accessible at the tourist centre, with a shuttle service to the castle.

To get to the location, take a train to Andria or Barletta and then take a local bus or cab from there.

• The closest airport is Bari Karol Wojtyła, located around 1.5 hours away.

Cost:

● Entry prices are around €10 per person, with reductions for children, students, and elderly. Guided tours are offered at an extra cost.

Basilica of San Nicola, Bari

What to Explore:

● Historical significance: The Basilica di San Nicola is a highly respected pilgrimage destination in Italy. It holds Saint Nicholas' relics (known as Santa Claus in popular culture).

The basilica is a stunning example of Romanesque architecture, with magnificent arches, beautiful carvings, and a tranquil crypt.

● Visit the crypt to view Saint Nicholas' relics, a popular destination for Catholic and Orthodox pilgrims worldwide.

● Visit the neighbouring Museo Nicolaiano to learn about the basilica's history and religious importance.

How to get there:

● The basilica is situated in Bari's Old Town, about 20 minutes from Bari Airport. There is little parking accessible nearby.

● Travel by rail to Bari Centrale, then walk or take a cab to the basilica.

● Local buses link different areas of Bari to the Old Town.

• The closest airport is Bari Karol Wojtyła, which is about 25 minutes away by vehicle or rail.

Cost:

● Admission to the basilica is free, although contributions are appreciated. The museum admission price ranges between €3 and €5.

Lecce's Baroque Churches and Historical Centre

What to Explore:

● Lecce's historical centre has exquisite Baroque architecture. Must-see churches are the Basilica di Santa Croce, the Duomo di Lecce, and the Chiesa di Sant'Irene.

● The Piazza del Duomo is a stunning plaza with elegant architecture like as the cathedral, bell tower, and bishop's residence.

● Visit the well-preserved Roman Amphitheater at Piazza Sant'Oronzo, a reminder of Lecce's Roman heritage.

● Craft stores: Lecce is well-known for its papier-mâché art, with workshops and stores located around the city.

● Evening strolls: The lit streets of Lecce's medieval centre provide a magnificent environment ideal for leisurely walks.

How to get there:

By car, Lecce is about 2 hours from Bari and 40 minutes from Brindisi. Parking is accessible outside the historical centre.

● Lecce's rail station provides easy access to Bari and other Puglia towns. The historical centre is a 10-minute walk from the station.

● Regional buses connect Lecce to other towns and cities in Puglia.

● The nearest airport is Brindisi Salento, which is about 40 minutes away by car or bus.

Cost:

● Free access to the historical centre and several churches. Entry prices for various sights, such as the Basilica di Santa Croce or the Roman Amphitheater, run from €2 and €6.

Each location provides a unique experience, from Alberobello's charming Trulli cottages to the majestic Castel del Monte, Bari's contemplative Basilica di San Nicola, and Lecce's stunning Baroque architecture. These renowned sites are must-sees for visitors visiting Puglia interested in history, culture, and architectural grandeur.

Natural Wonders.

Gargano National Park: A Paradise in Puglia

Nestled in the northernmost part of Puglia, Gargano National Park (*Parco Nazionale del Gargano*) is a breathtaking blend of pristine nature, ancient history, and vibrant biodiversity. Spanning over 120,000 hectares, this park is often referred to as the "Spur of the Italian Boot" due to its location and shape. It offers visitors a stunning array of landscapes, from dense forests and dramatic cliffs to sandy beaches and mystical caves.

Whether you're an adventurer, a nature lover, or someone seeking tranquility, Gargano National Park promises an unforgettable experience. Let's dive into everything this park has to offer.

What to Explore in Gargano National Park

The Umbra Forest (Foresta Umbra)

The heart of Gargano National Park is the **Umbra Forest**, a UNESCO World Heritage Site and one of Italy's oldest and most untouched forests. Walking through its dense, ancient beech trees feels like stepping into another world. Trails of varying difficulty wind through the forest, allowing you to explore hidden waterfalls, serene ponds, and a rich ecosystem of flora and fauna.

What to see:

- Centuries-old trees, including beech, oak, and maple.
- Wild animals such as deer, foxes, and badgers.
- Over 65 species of birds, including the elusive woodpecker.

Activities:
- Hiking and cycling trails.
- Guided nature walks.
- Visiting the small forest museum to learn about its biodiversity.

Coastal Cliffs and Beaches

Gargano is famous for its stunning coastline, where dramatic white cliffs meet the turquoise waters of the Adriatic Sea. The coastal scenery is dotted with secluded coves, sandy beaches, and unique sea caves.

Top Spots:

- **Baia delle Zagare:** A postcard-perfect beach known for its crystal-clear waters and limestone sea stacks.
- **Vieste Beaches:** Sandy stretches with shallow waters, perfect for families.
- **Sea Caves (Grotte Marine):** Accessible by boat tours from Vieste, these caves feature fascinating rock formations and emerald waters.
- **Activities:**

- Snorkeling and diving to explore the marine life.
- Kayaking along the cliffs.
- Sunset boat tours for a romantic experience.

Monte Sant'Angelo

Perched atop a hill, **Monte Sant'Angelo** is a charming medieval town with deep religious significance. It is home to the **Sanctuary of Monte Sant'Angelo**, a UNESCO World Heritage Site and one of the oldest Christian pilgrimage sites in Europe.

- **What to see:**
- The sanctuary's grotto, where St. Michael is said to have appeared.
- The medieval streets lined with traditional whitewashed houses.
- The Norman Castle, offering panoramic views of the surrounding landscape.

Tremiti Islands

Just off the coast of Gargano lies the **Tremiti Islands**, a small archipelago known for its crystal-clear waters and unspoiled beauty. The islands are a paradise for divers and snorkelers.

What to do:
- Visit **San Domino**, known for its lush pine forests and beaches.
- Explore **San Nicola**, home to ancient monasteries and historic ruins.
- Dive to explore shipwrecks and coral reefs.

Traditional Villages

Gargano is dotted with quaint villages that exude charm and authenticity.

- **Vico del Gargano:** Known as the "Village of Love," with its romantic alleys and citrus groves.
- **Peschici:** A picturesque village perched on a cliff, offering stunning sea views and delicious seafood.

What to Expect in Gargano National Park

Diverse Landscapes

- Gargano offers an unparalleled variety of terrains, from lush forests to rugged coastlines, sandy beaches to limestone plateaus.

Rich History

- The park is steeped in history, with ancient pilgrimage routes, medieval towns, and archaeological sites.

Local Cuisine
- expect to indulge in Puglian delicacies such as fresh seafood, handmade pasta like orecchiette, and citrus fruits from local groves. Don't miss the local olive oil and wines.

Wildlife Encounters
- Birdwatchers will delight in spotting peregrine falcons, eagles, and other rare species. Wildlife enthusiasts may encounter deer, foxes, and wild boars.

Mild Mediterranean Climate

- he park enjoys warm summers and mild winters, making it a year-round destination.

Parco Nazionale del Gargano
Province of Foggia, Italy

4.6 ★★★★★ 19,845 reviews

View larger map

Directions

Parco Nazionale
del Gargano

Gargano National Park

SCAN THE QR CODE
1. Open your device's camera app.
2. Align the QR code within the camera frame.
3. Wait for the code to be recognized.
4. Check the displayed notification or link.
5. Tap to access the linked content or information.

How to Get to Gargano National Park

By Air

- The nearest airport is **Bari Karol Wojtyła Airport**, approximately 200 km (124 miles) from the park. From the airport, you can rent a car or take a train to reach the Gargano area.

By Train

- The **Italian national railway** connects major cities to Foggia, the gateway to Gargano. From Foggia, local trains and buses provide access to park towns like Vieste, Peschici, and Monte Sant'Angelo.

By Car

- Driving is the most convenient way to explore Gargano. From Bari, take the A14 motorway toward Foggia, then follow signs to the Gargano peninsula. Roads within the park are scenic but can be narrow and winding, so drive cautiously.

By Ferry

- To visit the Tremiti Islands, ferries depart from **Vieste**, **Peschici**, and **Rodi Garganico**.

Costs and Budgeting

- **Park Entry**
  Gargano National Park does not charge an entry fee, but some attractions within the park, such as museums or guided tours, may have costs.

Accommodation

- Budget: €40–€60 per night (guesthouses, hostels).
- Mid-range: €70–€120 per night (hotels, agriturismo stays).
- Luxury: €150+ per night (resorts, villas).

Activities

- Guided hikes: €10–€20 per person.
- Boat tours to sea caves: €20–€50 per person.
- Ferry to Tremiti Islands: €25–€40 round trip.

Food

- Dining in Gargano is reasonably priced, with meals ranging from €10–€25 per person at local restaurants.

Transportation

- Car rentals: €30–€50 per day.
- Local buses: €1.50–€3 per trip.

Alimini Lakes

Alimini Lakes: A Tranquil Natural Escape in Puglia

The **Alimini Lakes**, or *Laghi Alimini*, are one of Puglia's most enchanting natural landscapes. Located just a few kilometers from Otranto, these twin lakes—**Alimini Grande** and **Alimini Piccolo**—offer a serene escape surrounded by lush greenery, pristine beaches, and unique wildlife. These lakes are a haven for nature lovers, birdwatchers, and outdoor enthusiasts seeking tranquility and breathtaking scenery.

What to Explore at Alimini Lakes

Alimini Grande

- The larger of the two lakes, **Alimini Grande**, is connected to the Adriatic Sea. Its brackish waters create a unique ecosystem, making it a hotspot for wildlife.

What to see:
- Migratory birds like herons, flamingos, and cormorants.
- Crystal-clear waters surrounded by dense vegetation.

Activities:
- Kayaking and canoeing to explore the lake's waters.
- Hiking around the lake on well-marked trails.

Alimini Piccolo

- Also known as **Fontanelle**, this smaller lake is freshwater and fed by underground springs.

What to see:
- A vibrant ecosystem of fish, amphibians, and aquatic plants.
- Panoramic views of the surrounding countryside.

Activities:
- Photography of the picturesque landscapes.
- Birdwatching for rare and endemic species.

Beaches Near Alimini Lakes

The Alimini Lakes are surrounded by some of Puglia's most stunning beaches, making it a perfect destination for combining nature and relaxation.

Top Beaches:
- **Baia dei Turchi:** A secluded, unspoiled https://www.canva.com/design/DAGbBZ2cqvw/YxygQgqZvKtdd1iAux28Ww/edit?utm_content=DAGbBZ2cqvw&utm_campaign=designshare&utm_medium=link2&utm_source=sharebutton with soft sand and turquoise waters.
- **Torre Sant'Andrea:** Known for its dramatic sea stacks and crystal-clear waters.

Activities:
- Swimming, sunbathing, and snorkeling.
- Exploring the nearby sea caves.

Trails and Surrounding Nature

- The area around the lakes offers several walking and cycling trails through pine forests, Mediterranean scrub, and olive groves.

What to expect:
- Scenic trails with views of both lakes and the sea.
- Opportunities to see wildflowers and butterflies in abundance.

What to Expect at Alimini Lakes

Tranquility and Nature

- The Alimini Lakes provide a peaceful retreat away from bustling tourist areas. The natural beauty is captivating and perfect for those seeking relaxation.

Rich Biodiversity

- The lakes are part of a protected area and are home to a variety of wildlife, making it a paradise for birdwatchers and nature photographers.

Crystal-Clear Waters

- Whether you're exploring the lakes themselves or the nearby beaches, expect pristine waters ideal for swimming and water sports.

Seasonal Beauty

- The lakes are stunning year-round, but spring and early summer offer the best opportunities to see flowers in bloom and migratory birds.

How to Get to Alimini Lakes

By Air

- The nearest airport is **Brindisi Airport**, approximately 90 km (56 miles) away. From there, you can rent a car or take a train to Otranto.

By Train

- Take a train to **Otranto**, the nearest town to the lakes. From Otranto, buses or taxis can take you to the Alimini area.

By Car

- Driving is the most convenient way to reach the lakes. From Lecce, follow the SS16 highway toward Otranto, and then take the coastal road to the lakes. Parking is available near the site.

By Bike

- For a more eco-friendly option, rent a bike in Otranto and ride along the scenic coastal trails leading to the lakes.

Costs and Budgeting

- **Entry Fee**
  There is no official entry fee to visit the Alimini Lakes, but guided tours or certain activities like kayaking may have costs.

Activities

- Kayak rentals: €10–€20 per hour.
- Guided birdwatching tours: €15–€30 per person.

Accommodation Nearby

- Budget: €40–€70 per night (camping or guesthouses).
- Mid-range: €80–€120 per night (local B&Bs or small hotels).
- Luxury: €150+ per night (resorts and villas near Otranto).
- **Dining Options**
  Nearby restaurants offer local Puglian cuisine, including fresh seafood and pasta dishes. Expect to pay €15–€30 per person for a meal.

Caves of Castellana

Caves of Castellana: A Journey into Puglia's Subterranean Wonder

The Caves of Castellana (*Grotte di Castellana*) are among Puglia's most remarkable natural attractions. Located in the Itria Valley, these limestone caves span over 3 kilometers, boasting spectacular stalactites, stalagmites, and underground galleries. Discovered in 1938, they offer a mesmerizing glimpse into a hidden world sculpted by nature over millions of years.

What to Explore at the Caves of Castellana

La Grave

- The first and largest cavern you'll encounter, it is an open-air sinkhole that reaches a depth of 60 meters (197 feet).

What to see:
- Stunning sunlight filtering through the sinkhole.
- Ancient rock formations and vibrant mosses.

White Cave (Grotta Bianca)

- Known as the most beautiful and radiant chamber in the cave system, the White Cave is adorned with dazzling white alabaster formations.
- What to see:
- Glittering stalactites and stalagmites resembling works of art.
- A pristine, ethereal atmosphere.

Corridor of Wonders

- A long passage filled with intricate rock formations that showcase the power of water and time.
- What to see:
- Sculptural stalagmites resembling candles and columns.
- Fossils embedded in the walls, offering glimpses into prehistoric life.

Other Highlights

- Black Cavern: A chamber with dark, dramatic features.
- The Owl's Cave: Named for its rock formations that resemble owls.
- The Desert Corridor: A drier section of the caves with unique geological formations.

What to Expect at the Caves of Castellana

Breathtaking Natural Formations

- Marvel at stalactites and stalagmites in an array of colors and shapes.
- Witness underground rivers, pools, and fossils that tell the story of the Earth's evolution.

Guided Tours

- Knowledgeable guides explain the history, geology, and legends associated with the caves.
- Tours are offered in multiple languages, including English.

Temperature and Atmosphere

- The caves remain cool year-round, with an average temperature of 16°C (61°F). Wear comfortable shoes and bring a light jacket.

Photography Opportunities

- Capture the beauty of the caves, but note that flash photography may not be permitted to preserve the delicate environment.

How to Get to the Caves of Castellana

By Air

- The nearest airport is Bari Karol Wojtyła Airport, approximately 50 km (31 miles) away. From there, you can rent a car or take public transport.

By Train

- Take a train to Castellana Grotte Station on the Ferrovie del Sud Est (FSE) line. From the station, the caves are a short taxi ride away.

By Car

- From Bari or Brindisi, follow the SS16 highway and take the exit for Castellana Grotte. Ample parking is available near the site.

By Bus

- Public buses run from nearby cities like Bari, Monopoli, and Alberobello to Castellana Grotte.

Costs and Budgeting

Entry Fees

- Short tour (1 km): €18 per adult.
- Full tour (3 km): €20 per adult.
- Discounts are available for children, seniors, and groups.

Guided Tours

- Included in the ticket price. Private tours may be available for an additional fee.

Extras

- Audioguides: €5 (optional for a self-paced experience).
- Souvenir shops offer geological books, postcards, and unique mementos.

Accommodation Nearby

- Budget: €50–€70 per night (local B&Bs or guesthouses).
- Mid-range: €80–€120 per night (hotels in Castellana Grotte).
- Luxury: €150+ per night (boutique hotels and countryside resorts).

Dining Options

- Several restaurants near the caves serve traditional Puglian cuisine, including handmade pasta and fresh seafood. Expect to pay €15–€30 per person for a meal.

Tips for Visitors

- Wear sturdy, non-slip footwear, as the cave floors can be uneven and damp.
- Arrive early, especially during peak tourist season, to avoid long lines.
- Check for special events like night tours or concerts inside the caves.

The Poetic Grotto

The Poetic Grotto (*Grotta della Poesia*) is one of Puglia's most enchanting natural wonders. Located in **Roca Vecchia**, a coastal area near Melendugno, this karstic sea cave has earned its poetic name due to its unparalleled beauty and mythical associations. The turquoise waters, ancient ruins, and legends surrounding the grotto make it a must-visit destination for history buffs, nature lovers, and adventurers alike.

What to Explore at The Poetic Grotto

The Main Sinkhole

- A natural limestone pool filled with crystal-clear, emerald-green waters.

What to see:
- Spectacular underwater rock formations.
- The perfect blend of sunlight and water reflections creating a magical atmosphere.

Activities:
- Swimming and cliff diving (only for experienced swimmers).
- Snorkeling to explore the marine life.

The Smaller Grotto

- A nearby smaller cave connected to the main grotto by an underground passage.

What to see:
- Unique geological formations and a more secluded swimming area.

Activities:
- Exploring the passageways.

- Quiet relaxation and photography.

Archaeological Sites

- Ancient ruins surrounding the grotto tell stories of Puglia's rich history.

What to see:
- Remnants of Messapian settlements.
- Carvings and inscriptions on the cave walls believed to be dedications to gods.

The Adriatic Coastline

- The surrounding area offers stunning views of the Adriatic Sea and rugged cliffs.

What to see:
- Endless vistas of turquoise waters meeting the horizon.
- Rocky outcrops and coastal trails.

What to Expect at The Poetic Grotto

A Natural Swimming Paradise

- The grotto is perfect for swimming, with its refreshing waters and natural beauty providing a tranquil experience.

Rich Mythology and Legends

- According to local legend, the grotto was a place where poets and writers were inspired by its beauty, hence its poetic name.

Breathtaking Scenery

- Expect awe-inspiring views that are both picturesque and dramatic, perfect for photography enthusiasts.

Seasonal Popularity

- Summer is the busiest time, with tourists flocking to enjoy the waters. Early mornings or evenings are ideal for a quieter visit.

How to Get to The Poetic Grotto

By Air

- The nearest airport is **Brindisi Airport**, about 75 km (47 miles) away. From there, rent a car or take public transport to Melendugno.

By Train

- Take a train to **Lecce**, the nearest major city, and then continue by car or bus to Roca Vecchia.

By Car

- Driving is the most convenient way to reach the grotto. From Lecce, take the SS16 highway and follow signs for Melendugno and Roca Vecchia. Parking is available nearby.

By Bus

- Seasonal buses operate from Lecce to Roca Vecchia during peak tourist months.

Costs and Budgeting

Entry Fee

- Visiting the grotto is typically free, but some guided tours may have costs.

Activities

- Guided snorkeling tours: €15–€25 per person.
- Boat tours of the coastline: €20–€50 per person.

Accommodation Nearby

- Budget: €40–€60 per night (local guesthouses).
- Mid-range: €80–€120 per night (B&Bs and boutique hotels).
- Luxury: €150+ per night (coastal resorts).

Dining Options

- Enjoy local seafood specialties and Puglian dishes in nearby restaurants. Expect to pay €15–€30 per person for a meal.

Tips for Visitors

- Bring water shoes to navigate the rocky terrain safely.
- Arrive early to secure a spot, especially during peak season.
- Respect the environment—avoid littering and damaging the natural formations.
- Consider booking a guided tour to learn about the grotto's history and legends.

Picturesque towns

Otranto: The Jewel of the Adriatic

Nestled along Puglia's scenic coastline, **Otranto** is a charming seaside town that combines historical intrigue, stunning landscapes, and vibrant culture. Known as the easternmost town in Italy, it offers visitors a mix of ancient history, UNESCO-listed landmarks, and breathtaking seaside views. Whether you're exploring its medieval streets or relaxing on its pristine beaches, Otranto is a must-visit destination.

What to Explore in Otranto

Otranto Cathedral (Cathedral of Santa Maria Annunziata)

- A masterpiece of Romanesque architecture, the cathedral is the heart of Otranto's history.

What to see:
- The **Mosaic Floor:** A 12th-century mosaic depicting the Tree of Life, mythical creatures, and biblical scenes.
- The **Crypt:** A tranquil underground space with columns and frescoes.
- The **Chapel of the Martyrs:** Dedicated to the 800 martyrs of Otranto who resisted Ottoman invaders in 1480.

Aragonese Castle (Castello Aragonese)

- This imposing fortress played a pivotal role in defending Otranto from invaders.

What to see:
- Massive walls and towers offering panoramic views of the town and sea.
- The interior museum showcasing historical artifacts and exhibitions.
- Walking paths along the moat for a glimpse into medieval defensive strategies.

Porta Alfonsina

- The ancient gateway to Otranto, leading into the old town's labyrinthine streets.

What to see:
- Narrow alleys lined with whitewashed buildings and vibrant flowers.
- Local artisan shops selling pottery, textiles, and souvenirs.

Lungomare degli Eroi (Seafront Promenade)

- A scenic walkway along the Adriatic Sea.

What to see:
- Stunning views of the turquoise waters and harbor.
- Cafés and gelaterias perfect for relaxing and enjoying local treats.

Beaches Around Otranto

- Otranto is surrounded by some of Puglia's most beautiful beaches.

What to explore:
- **Baia dei Turchi:** A secluded beach with crystal-clear waters and soft sands.
- **Torre dell'Orso:** Known for its dramatic cliffs and twin rock formations, the "Two Sisters."
- **Alimini Beaches:** Long stretches of fine sand backed by pine forests.

San Pietro Church (Chiesa di San Pietro)

- A small Byzantine church adorned with vibrant frescoes.

What to see:
- Detailed depictions of biblical scenes in a serene atmosphere.

What to Expect in Otranto

Rich History

- A melting pot of cultures, Otranto reflects Greek, Roman, Byzantine, and Norman influences.

Charming Old Town

- Winding streets, lively squares, and a warm, welcoming atmosphere.

Stunning Natural Beauty

- Otranto boasts dramatic cliffs, azure waters, and golden beaches.

Seasonal Vibrancy

- Summer is lively with tourists, while spring and autumn offer a quieter, more relaxed experience.

How to Get to Otranto

By Air

- The nearest airport is **Brindisi Airport**, located about 95 km (59 miles) away. From there, rent a car or use public transportation.

By Train

- Take a train to **Lecce**, then connect to Otranto via the Ferrovie del Sud Est (FSE) train line.

By Car

- From Lecce, follow the SS16 and SP366 highways directly to Otranto. Parking is available near the town center and beaches.

By Bus

- Seasonal buses run from Lecce to Otranto, making it an accessible option during peak tourist months.

Costs and Budgeting

Accommodation Options

- **Budget**: €40–€60 per night (hostels or small guesthouses).
- **Mid-range:** €80–€120 per night (B&Bs and boutique hotels).
- **Luxury**: €150+ per night (seafront resorts and high-end accommodations).

Dining

- Local restaurants serve fresh seafood, orecchiette pasta, and regional wines. Expect to pay €15–€35 per person.

Activities

- **Entry to Otranto Cathedral:** Free or donation-based.
- **Aragonese Castle:** €8–€10 per person.
- **Guided tours:** €20–€40 per person, depending on duration and focus.

Tips for Visitors

- Wear comfortable shoes for walking the cobblestone streets.
- Bring swimwear to enjoy the beaches and coastal waters.
- Visit early in the day to explore popular landmarks without large crowds.
- Try local specialties like **pasticciotto** (a custard-filled pastry) and **Negroamaro wine**.

Polignano A Mare

Polignano a Mare, located on the Adriatic coast of Puglia, is a breathtaking coastal town known for its dramatic cliffside setting, crystal-clear waters, and rich history. The town's unique architecture, perched on limestone cliffs, offers stunning views of the sea, making it one of the most picturesque destinations in Italy. With its charming old town, beautiful beaches, and vibrant atmosphere, Polignano a Mare is an unforgettable destination for travelers.

What to Explore in Polignano a Mare

The Lama Monachile Beach

- A small yet stunning beach located between two cliffs, offering serene waters and a unique landscape.

What to see:
- The beach is surrounded by dramatic cliffs, creating a secluded and intimate atmosphere.
- The view from the cliffs above offers one of the most iconic vistas in Polignano.

The Historic Old Town

- Wander through narrow, cobblestone streets lined with whitewashed houses and vibrant flowers.

What to see:
- The **Piazza Vittorio Emanuele**, the main square, filled with cafés and lively restaurants.
- The **Church of St. Mary of the Assumption (Chiesa di Santa Maria Assunta)** with its beautiful Baroque-style architecture.
- The **Statue of Domenico Modugno**, the famous singer who was born in Polignano, located by the sea.

Grotta Palazzese (Palazzese Cave Restaurant)

- One of the most exclusive and unique dining experiences in the world, located inside a sea cave.

What to see:
- The stunning cave interior, where diners enjoy their meals overlooking the Adriatic Sea.

Activities:
- Dining in this historic cave restaurant, especially at sunset, offers a magical experience.

Ponte Borbonico

- A historical bridge that spans the Lama Monachile creek, connecting different parts of the town.

What to see:
- The beautiful stone arch bridge and its role in Polignano's history.
- Panoramic views of the surrounding cliffs and sea.

The Sea Grottos (Grotte di Polignano)

- The cliffs surrounding Polignano are home to several sea caves.

What to explore:
- Take a boat tour to discover these hidden caves, including Grotta Azzurra, Grotta delle Rondinelle, and Grotta Palazzese.
- Enjoy snorkeling in the clear waters of the caves.

The Beaches of Polignano a Mare

- Beyond Lama Monachile, there are several beautiful beaches along the coast.

What to explore:
- **Spiaggia di San Vito:** A peaceful sandy beach just outside the town, perfect for a relaxing day by the sea.
- **Cala Porto:** A small cove with crystal-clear waters, ideal for swimming and sunbathing.

What to Expect in Polignano a Mare

Breathtaking Views

- Expect panoramic vistas of the Adriatic Sea, dramatic cliffs, and idyllic beaches that make this town one of the most photogenic in Italy.

Charming Atmosphere

- The historic center is peaceful and picturesque, with plenty of cafes, gelaterias, and boutique shops. The town is known for its welcoming, relaxed vibe.

Rich Cultural Heritage

- Polignano a Mare is steeped in history, with influences from ancient Greeks, Romans, and Normans. The town is famous for its medieval old town and artistic traditions.

Busy During Summer

- Expect larger crowds during the summer months, with the town bustling with tourists. If you prefer a quieter visit, consider traveling in spring or fall.

How to Get to Polignano a Mare

By Air

- The nearest airport is **Bari Karol Wojtyła Airport**, approximately 40 km (25 miles) away. From there, you can rent a car, take a train, or use a bus to reach Polignano a Mare.

By Train

- Polignano a Mare has its own train station, which is well connected to Bari and other towns in Puglia. Trains are frequent and a convenient option for travelers.

By Car

- Polignano a Mare is easily accessible by car from Bari, driving south along the SS16 highway. Parking is available near the town center, but spaces can be limited during peak season.

By Bus

- Buses connect Polignano a Mare to Bari, Monopoli, and other nearby towns. During the summer, additional seasonal buses operate to accommodate tourists.

Costs and Budgeting

Accommodation

- **Budget**: €40–€70 per night (hostels, guesthouses, or smaller hotels).
- **Mid-range:** €80–€150 per night (B&Bs, boutique hotels).
- **Luxury**: €200+ per night (cliffside resorts or hotels with ocean views).

Dining

- **Casual dining:** €15–€30 per person for traditional Italian dishes like orecchiette and seafood.
- **Fine dining (like Grotta Palazzese):** €80–€150 per person for a unique dining experience.

Activities

- **Boat tours of the sea grottos:** €20–€40 per person.
- **Guided tours of the historic old town:** €10–€20 per person.

Tips for Visitors

- **Wear Comfortable Footwear:** The streets of Polignano a Mare are cobbled and can be uneven, so sturdy shoes are ideal for exploring.
- **Swim Early or Late:** During peak tourist season, the beaches can become crowded, so arrive early or later in the afternoon for a more peaceful experience.
- **Take a Boat Tour:** The sea grottos are a must-see and best explored by boat, with several local operators offering guided tours.
- **Book Ahead for Restaurants:** Particularly for Grotta Palazzese, reservations are essential due to its exclusivity and popularity.
- **Explore Beyond the Beaches:** While the beaches are a big draw, don't miss exploring the charming old town and nearby historical sites.

Matera

Matera, located in the region of Basilicata, is one of Italy's most unique and fascinating destinations. Known for its ancient cave dwellings, winding stone streets, and rich history, Matera is often referred to as the "City of Stones." It has been continuously inhabited for thousands of years and is a UNESCO World Heritage site. The city's ethereal charm, ancient architecture, and breathtaking views make it a must-visit location for history buffs, nature lovers, and those seeking a unique Italian experience.

What to Explore in Matera

Sassi di Matera (The Stones of Matera)

- Matera's most famous feature, the **Sassi**, are ancient cave dwellings carved into the limestone rock.

What to see:
- **Sasso Caveoso and Sasso Barisano:** These two districts are home to the majority of the cave dwellings, with homes, churches, and narrow alleys.
- **Cave Churches:** Explore rock-cut churches like the **Church of San Pietro Barisano** and **Santa Maria de Idris**, which date back to the 9th and 10th centuries.
- **Casa Grotta di Vico Solitario:** A traditional cave house that provides a glimpse into how the inhabitants once lived.

Matera Cathedral (Cattedrale di Matera)

- Located at the highest point of Matera, the cathedral is a stunning example of Romanesque architecture.

What to see:
- The cathedral's intricate facades and stunning interior with beautiful frescoes.
- **The Crypt of the Original Sin:** An evocative, 9th-century cave church with remarkable frescoes depicting biblical scenes.

Palazzo Lanfranchi and Museo Nazionale d'Arte Medievale e Moderna

- A beautiful 17th-century palace that now houses a museum dedicated to the region's medieval and modern art.

What to see:
- The museum's exhibitions of local artworks, sculptures, and religious artifacts.
- The panoramic terrace offering a fantastic view of the Sassi and the surrounding countryside.

The Belvedere di Murgia Timone

- A scenic viewpoint that offers one of the most breathtaking panoramic views of Matera and its surroundings.

What to explore:
- A perfect spot to take in the unique cityscape of ancient cave dwellings against the dramatic landscape.
- The nearby **Murgia National Park**, home to ancient cave settlements and prehistoric remains.

The Crypt of the Original Sin (Crypta del Peccato Originale)

- Known as the "Sistine Chapel of Puglia," this cave church is decorated with vibrant frescoes depicting the creation of man, the fall of Adam and Eve, and scenes from the Old Testament.

What to see:
- The vivid frescoes, some of the oldest and best-preserved in Italy, created by Byzantine and medieval artists.
- The well-preserved and atmospheric setting of the cave church.

The Rupestrian Churches

- Scattered across the Murgia plateau and surrounding areas, these rock-cut churches are a testament to Matera's ancient Christian heritage.

What to explore:

- **Church of Santa Maria della Valle** and **Church of San Nicola dei Greci** are notable examples that can be visited on foot or by bike.

What to Expect in Matera

Ancient Atmosphere

- Matera's Sassi district feels like stepping back in time, with its ancient cave dwellings, winding alleys, and traditional stone houses. The city maintains its old-world charm while embracing modern touches.

Stunning Views

- From the Belvedere di Murgia Timone to the panoramic terrace at Palazzo Lanfranchi, Matera offers incredible vistas of the surrounding landscape, particularly during sunrise and sunset.

Rich History and Culture

- Matera's deep historical roots, spanning thousands of years, are evident in its architecture, churches, and cave dwellings. Visitors can trace the evolution of human settlements in the region from prehistoric to medieval times.

Quiet Charm

- Matera is quieter than other popular Italian destinations, making it an excellent spot for visitors seeking peace and reflection. The town's peaceful atmosphere makes it a relaxing getaway, especially in the off-season.

How to Get to Matera

By Air

- The nearest airport is **Bari Karol Wojtyła Airport**, located approximately 65 km (40 miles) from Matera. From the airport, you can rent a car, take a bus, or hire a taxi to reach the city.

By Train

- Matera has a train station connected to Bari and other towns in Puglia, though trains are less frequent. Alternatively, take a train to Bari, then connect to Matera by bus or hire a car.

By Car

- Matera is easily accessible by car via the **SS7** or **SS99** highways from Bari. The town is well-connected by road and offers parking near the city center.

By Bus

- Buses connect Matera to nearby cities like Bari, Altamura, and Taranto. Several bus companies operate regular routes to Matera, especially during the tourist season.

Costs and Budgeting

- **Accommodation**

- Budget: €40–€70 per night (guesthouses, hostels, and budget hotels).

- Mid-range: €80–€150 per night (B&Bs and boutique hotels).
- Luxury: €150+ per night (cave hotels and upscale accommodations).

Dining

- Casual dining: €10–€25 per person for traditional dishes such as **orecchiette** pasta and **lamb** dishes.
- Fine dining: €30–€50 per person for a multi-course meal in one of Matera's renowned restaurants.

Activities

- Entry to Matera Cathedral: Free, although donations are encouraged.
- Museum Entry (Palazzo Lanfranchi): €5–€10 per person.
- Guided tours of the Sassi and nearby caves: €20–€30 per person.

Tips for Visitors

- **Wear Comfortable Shoes:** Matera's streets are narrow, cobbled, and often steep. Comfortable shoes are essential for exploring the old town.
- **Book Cave Hotels in Advance:** Matera is famous for its unique cave hotels. Booking in advance is recommended, especially in peak seasons.
- **Visit the Cave Churches:** Many of the cave churches are still active places of worship, and visiting during mass or a service can provide a unique cultural experience.
- **Best Time to Visit:** The best times to visit Matera are spring and autumn, when the weather is mild and the city is less crowded. Summer can be hot, and the city can get busy with tourists.

Locorotondo

Locorotondo, located in the heart of the Itria Valley in the Puglia region, is often considered one of the most picturesque towns in Italy. Renowned for its whitewashed trulli houses, winding streets, and scenic hilltop views, Locorotondo offers visitors a mix of authentic Southern Italian charm, history, and culture. This circular town, whose name means "round place," is a gem of the Puglia region, ideal for those seeking an off-the-beaten-path experience in Italy.

What to Explore in Locorotondo

The Historic Center

The town's historic center is a maze of narrow streets and alleys, with traditional whitewashed buildings adorned with colorful flowers and vines.

What to see:

Piazza Vittorio Emanuele II: The main square, with its elegant cafes, is perfect for people-watching and enjoying the relaxed pace of life.
Charming Streets: Explore streets like Via Nardelli and Via Morelli, where you can find small shops selling local products, including wine, olive oil, and artisanal crafts.

Trulli Houses

Like its neighbors Alberobello and Cisternino, Locorotondo is known for its **trulli**—small, cone-shaped stone houses. While most of the trulli are located outside the town center, there are several to see within walking distance.

What to see:
Trulli in the Countryside: Take a walk or bike ride through the countryside to see trulli scattered across the rolling hills of the Itria Valley.

Trulli Architecture: Admire the unique and historic construction techniques of the trulli, with their dry-stone walls and conical roofs.

Church of San Giorgio

This stunning church, located at the highest point of Locorotondo, is one of the town's main landmarks.

What to see:

The church's baroque-style façade, its rich interior with beautiful frescoes, and the stunning views over the surrounding countryside.

The Belvedere (Panoramic Viewpoint)

One of the best spots in Locorotondo for panoramic views of the Itria Valley.

What to explore:
The viewpoint offers a sweeping view of the town's characteristic trulli houses and the lush, green valley below.
The rolling hills and vineyards create a stunning landscape, perfect for photographs, particularly during sunrise and sunset.

The Wine Route (Strada del Vino)

Locorotondo is part of the **Locorotondo DOC wine region**, and wine lovers will appreciate the local vineyards and wineries.

What to explore:

Take a guided wine tour to learn about the area's unique **white wine** made from the **Verdeca and Bianco d'Alessano** grapes.

Visit local wineries for tastings and enjoy the opportunity to purchase some of the region's finest wines directly from the producers.

The Mother Church of Saint George (Chiesa Madre di San Giorgio)

This historic church, dedicated to the town's patron saint, is an important symbol of Locorotondo.

What to see:
- Admire the church's ornate Baroque interior, complete with impressive altars and frescoes.
- Take in the stunning view of the valley from the church's bell tower.

The Olive Oil Museum (Museo dell'Olio)

- For those interested in the region's agricultural traditions, a visit to the **Olive Oil Museum** is a must.

What to see:
- Learn about the history of olive oil production in Puglia, from ancient methods to modern techniques.
- Explore the museum's displays of old olive presses, tools, and historical artifacts related to olive cultivation.

What to Expect in Locorotondo

A Quiet, Relaxed Atmosphere

- Locorotondo offers a laid-back, tranquil atmosphere, making it perfect for a relaxing getaway. The town is less crowded compared to other destinations in Puglia, providing visitors with a more authentic and peaceful experience.
- Expect to leisurely stroll through the charming streets, sip espresso at a café, and soak up the local lifestyle.

Breathtaking Views

- Whether you're gazing over the valley from the town's historic center or walking through the countryside surrounded by trulli, Locorotondo offers some of the most stunning vistas in Puglia.

Authentic Pugliese Cuisine

- Locorotondo's cuisine is a reflection of the local agricultural traditions, with an emphasis on fresh, seasonal ingredients. Expect to sample dishes made with olive oil, fresh vegetables, meats, and local cheeses.
- Try the **orecchiette** pasta, **Caciocavallo** cheese, and **local wines**. Don't miss the chance to dine in a traditional trattoria for an authentic experience.

Festivals and Local Events

- Locorotondo hosts a variety of local festivals and events throughout the year, celebrating everything from music and food to religious traditions.
- **La Festa di San Giorgio** (Saint George's Feast), held in late April or early May, is a major celebration for the town's patron saint, featuring parades, music, and fireworks.

How to Get to Locorotondo

By Air

- The nearest airport is **Bari Karol Wojtyła Airport**, about 60 km (37 miles) from Locorotondo. From there, you can take a bus, rent a car, or hire a taxi to reach the town.
- Alternatively, **Brindisi Airport** is approximately 90 km (56 miles) away, offering another access point for travelers.

By Train

- Locorotondo is well-connected by train to other towns in the region. The **Locorotondo train station** is located just outside the town center, with connections to **Alberobello**, **Bari**, and **Taranto**.
- The **Ferrovia Appulo Lucana** line connects Locorotondo to nearby towns, making it easy to travel by train.

By Car

- Locorotondo is easily accessible by car, located just off the **SS172** highway that runs through the Itria Valley. It is well-signposted and can be reached from **Alberobello**, **Cisternino**, or **Martina Franca**.

By Bus

- Buses operate regularly from nearby towns like **Alberobello**, **Cisternino**, and **Martina Franca**. The **Fermata di Locorotondo** is the main bus station in the town.

Costs and Budgeting

Accommodation

- **Budget**: €40–€70 per night (guesthouses and budget hotels).
- **Mid-range:** €80–€150 per night (B&Bs and boutique hotels).
- **Luxury:** €150+ per night (upscale hotels and countryside retreats).

Dining

- **Casual dining**: €10–€25 per person for local dishes like **orecchiette** pasta and **lamb** dishes.
- **Fine dining:** €30–€50 per person for a full-course meal in a renowned restaurant.

Activities

- **Wine tastings:** €10–€20 per person for a tour of local vineyards.
- **Museum entry:** €3–€5 per person for the Olive Oil Museum and other local attractions.
- **Guided tours of the town**: €15–€30 per person for a walking tour.

Tips for Visitors

- **Explore the Countryside:** The area surrounding Locorotondo is beautiful, with vineyards, olive groves, and rolling hills. Renting a bike or taking a leisurely walk through the countryside is a great way to enjoy the region.

- **Visit in the Off-Season:** While Locorotondo is charming year-round, it is especially peaceful in the off-season (autumn and spring).
- **Enjoy the Local Wine:** The region is famous for its **Locorotondo DOC** wine, so be sure to visit a local winery and sample the white wine varieties.
- **Stay in a Trulli:** For a truly unique experience, consider staying in a traditional trullo. Some of the trulli are available as holiday rentals, providing an unforgettable experience.

Chapter 3. Getting There

By plane, train, bus, or car

Getting to Puglia By Air

Puglia is well-connected by air, with multiple international and regional airports providing convenient access to the area. Whether you're coming from another Italian city or visiting worldwide, flying into Puglia is a practical alternative.

Main Airports in Puglia

Bari Karol Wojtyła Airport (Aeroporto di Bari

Location: Approximately 8 kilometres northwest of Bari, the provincial capital.

Overview: Bari Airport is Puglia's biggest and busiest, handling both local and international flights. It has multiple direct flights from major European cities, making it a popular gateway for tourists. The airport is well-equipped with stores, restaurants, and services to guarantee a comfortable arrival.

Flights:

• Bari Airport has international flights to major European destinations including London, Frankfurt, Milan, and Rome.

• The airport serves regular domestic flights from major Italian cities such as Rome, Milan, and Naples.

How To Get To The City:

• The AMTAB bus service links the airport to Bari's city centre, taking around 30 minutes. The buses operate often, and tickets cost around €1.

• Taxis are widely accessible at the airport. A taxi to the city centre costs about €20-25 and takes around 20 minutes.

• Rental cars are available at the airport. Driving to the city centre or nearby regions is simple and takes around 20 minutes.

Brindisi's Papola Casale Airport

Location: Approximately 6 kilometres southwest of Brindisi.

Brindisi Airport is the second-largest international gateway into Puglia. It is smaller than Bari Airport but handles a wide range of international and local flights, mostly from European destinations. The airport is notably accessible for people travelling to southern Puglia, including Lecce, Otranto, and the Salento area.

Flights:

Brindisi Airport offers international flights to major European cities like London, Berlin, and Vienna.

• Regular domestic flights depart from Rome and Milan.

How To Get To The City:

The Autolinee Salento bus service links the airport with Brindisi's principal rail station. The travel takes around 15 minutes and tickets cost roughly €1.50.

• Taxi: Available outside the terminal. A cab to the city centre costs between €15 and €20 and takes around 15 minutes.

• Car rental firms are located at the airport. Driving to Brindisi's city centre takes around 15 minutes.

Foggia Gino Lisa Airport (Aeroporto Di Foggia)

Location: Approximately 4 kilometres from Foggia's city centre.

Overview: Foggia is a tiny airport that mostly serves regional aircraft around Italy. Although it has fewer international connections, it is a viable alternative if you are heading to northern Puglia or the surrounding districts.

Flights:

Foggia has minimal international connections but offers seasonal flights.

• The airport mostly serves Milan and Rome, with domestic flights.

How To Get To The City:

• Local buses link the airport with Foggia's major bus and rail terminals. The trip takes around 15 minutes.

• Taxi to the city centre costs around €10-15.

• Car rental options are provided at the airport, providing convenient access to Foggia and adjacent destinations.

Smaller airports and alternatives

Taranto-Grottaglie Airport (Aeroporto Di Taranto-Grottaglie)

While Taranto-Grottaglie Airport is largely utilized for military and freight aircraft, it also handles some commercial traffic, particularly charter planes. It is around 10 kilometres from Taranto and might be an alternative for visitors to the Ionian Coast.

Lecce Train Station (Stazione di Lecce)

Although Lecce does not have an airport, it is easily accessible by rail from Bari and Brindisi. Lecce is a popular tourist resort in southern Puglia, with most tourists arriving via Brindisi or Bari airports.

General Tips for Flying to Puglia

● Flight duration:

• Travel time from Rome to Bari: 1 hour.

• Travel time from Milan to Bari: 1 hour and 20 minutes.

• Travel time from London to Bari: 2 hours and 30 minutes.

• Travel time from Berlin to Brindisi: 2 hours and 20 minutes.

• Travel time from Vienna to Brindisi: 2 hours and 10 minutes.

● Low-cost airlines:

Many low-cost airlines, like as Ryanair and EasyJet, provide frequent flights to Bari and Brindisi from many European locations. Early booking might result in lower rates, particularly during high tourist seasons.

● Best time to fly:

The summer months (June through August) are the busiest, and flights might be more costly. Consider going during the shoulder seasons (April to May or September to October), when the weather is still beautiful but the crowds are less.

Flying into Puglia is a fantastic choice for tourists looking to discover the region's history, beaches, and culinary offerings. The combination of large airports in Bari and Brindisi, as well as smaller regional airports like Foggia, allows for convenient access from a variety of European and Italian locations.

Getting to Puglia via train

Travelling by rail to Puglia is a lovely and easy way to visit this wonderful area. Italy has a vast and well-connected rail network, making it simple to travel between major cities and villages, including those in Puglia. Whether you're visiting from another area of Italy or going within the region, the train may be a convenient and stress-free option.

Key Train Stations in Puglia

Bari Centrale

Bari Centrale is the principal rail station in Bari, Puglia's capital. It is situated in the city centre.

Overview: Bari Centrale serves as a key transportation hub for regional and national trains. It is well-linked to major cities in Italy, such as Milan, Rome, Naples, and Lecce, making it one of the most accessible stations in the area. The station has a variety of amenities, including shops, restaurants, and waiting places.

Train services:

• High-speed trains (Frecciarossa and Italo) link Bari Centrale with Rome (about 4 hours), Milan (7 hours), and Naples (2 hours).

• Regional trains (Regionale) link Bari with adjacent towns and cities in Puglia, including Lecce, Brindisi, and Polignano a Mare.

• Intercity Trains: Direct connections to other Italian cities, including Florence and Bologna.

How To Get To The City:

Bari Centrale is conveniently located among the city's major attractions. Taxis and buses are also available.

Lecce Train Station

Lecce Railway Station is located in the middle of Lecce, a large city in southern Puglia, sometimes known as the "Florence of the South."

Overview: Lecce is a renowned tourist destination owing to its spectacular baroque architecture, and the station offers great rail connections to the rest of Italy and Puglia. The station is well-equipped with contemporary facilities including ticket desks, waiting spaces, and cafés.

Train services:

• High-speed trains link Lecce to Bari in about 40 minutes. Services to Rome and Naples are slower and need one or two transfers.

• Lecce has regular regional train connections that link it to surrounding towns including Otranto, Brindisi, and Gallipoli.

• Intercity Trains: Lecce has links to Milan, Bologna, and Florence.

How To Get To The City:

The station is within walking distance of Lecce's historic centre, allowing you to explore the city immediately upon arrival. Taxis and buses are available for anyone heading deeper into the surrounding region.

Brindisi Train Station

Brindisi Railway Station is situated just outside Brindisi's city centre, on the shore.

Overview: Brindisi is an important port city and a significant transit hub for visitors to Puglia. The station offers both regional and interstate connections and is the primary train hub for people travelling to the Salento Peninsula.

Train services:

• High-speed trains link Brindisi to Bari in roughly an hour, with connections to important cities including Rome and Milan via changeover.

Brindisi has convenient regional rail connections to adjacent towns, including Lecce, Otranto, and Taranto.

• Intercity trains connect Brindisi to other areas of Italy but usually need one or two transfers.

How To Get To The City:

The station is about ten minutes by cab from the city centre. There are also local buses and trams that link the station to other sections of Brindisi.

Foggia Train Station

Foggia Railway Station is situated in the heart of Foggia, in northern Puglia.

Overview: Foggia serves as an important rail station for northern Puglia and links to other regions of southern Italy. It is particularly useful for those travelling to and from the Gargano Peninsula.

Train services:

• High-speed trains link Foggia to large cities like Milan and Rome, requiring just one or two stops.

• The station provides regular regional train services to places like Manfredonia, San Severo, and Bari.

☆ Foggia has excellent intercity train connections to cities in the south, such as Naples and Bari.

How To Get To The City:

The main core of Foggia is a short walk from the train station. Taxis and local buses are also available for those travelling to other parts of the city.

Train Travel Tips in Puglia

● Ticket options:

Tickets for high-speed trains (Frecciarossa and Italo) may be bought online, at the station, or via mobile applications. Regional rail tickets may also be bought on the day of travel. It is best to reserve high-speed trains in advance, particularly during busy travel seasons.

• Regional train prices vary from €5 to €20, depending on distance.

• High-speed trains cost between €25 and €50, depending on route and service class.

• Discounts are offered to elders, kids, and organizations. Rail passes, such as the Eurail Pass or InterRail Pass, may also help travellers save money and provide flexibility on several train excursions.

• Travel times:

From Bari to Lecce takes around 40 minutes by high-speed rail and 1 hour by regional train.

• The journey from Bari to Brindisi takes around 1 hour by regional or high-speed rail.

• The journey from Bari to Foggia takes around 2 hours by regional or intercity rail.

• High-speed rail travel time from Bari to Milan is around 7 hours.

• High-speed rail travel time from Bari to Rome is around 4 hours.

● Book tickets:

Tickets may be bought at stations or online from websites such as Trenitalia or Italo, which include complete timetables, ticket choices, and seat reservations.

● Scenic journeys:

Train travel in Puglia provides picturesque routes, particularly in the southern regions. The route from Bari to Lecce, for example, provides vistas of olive trees, vineyards, and seaside sceneries. It's an excellent way to enjoy the region's beauty without the stress of driving.

Benefits of Traveling by Train in Puglia

● Comfort and Convenience: Italian trains are renowned for their comfort, punctuality, and efficiency. High-speed trains include contemporary facilities like air conditioning, Wi-Fi, and food service, making lengthy travels more comfortable.

● Environmental Impact: Traveling by rail is a more environmentally responsible alternative than driving, lowering your carbon footprint while visiting the area.

● Ease of Access: Trains link Puglia's main cities and villages, with stations near city centres, reducing the need to navigate unfamiliar roads.

Trains are a cost-effective option for passengers due to their low rates and accessible discounts.

Travelling by rail is one of the greatest ways to visit Puglia, providing a practical, picturesque, and pleasant mode of transportation. Whether you're visiting from elsewhere in Italy or touring the area, Puglia's rail network makes it simple to get to all of the key locations and beyond.

Getting to Puglia by Bus

Many people, particularly those travelling from other parts of Italy or Europe, find that taking the bus to Puglia is a cheap and easy choice. Various regional and national firms run bus services to and throughout Puglia, offering a great alternative to railroads and planes. Buses are slower, but they provide more flexibility and cost-effective alternatives, particularly for longer journeys.

Key Bus Stations in Puglia

Bari Central Bus Station (Autostazione Bari Centrale).

Location: Near the Bari Centrale Train Station, in the centre of the city.

Overview: Bari is Puglia's capital and a major bus hub for the rest of the province and Italy. Bari's bus terminal is well-linked to neighbouring cities in Puglia and beyond. It is perfectly positioned for travellers coming by rail, with quick access to cabs, trams, and the city centre.

Bus services:

☆ Bari has a strong regional bus network that connects it to places including Lecce, Brindisi, Taranto, and Polignano a Mare.

• Long-distance buses link Bari to major Italian cities, including Rome, Naples, Milan, and Florence.

• International busses: Bari serves buses from several European countries, including Albania, Greece, and other Mediterranean locations.

How To Get To The City:

The bus terminal is a short walk from the Bari Centrale Train terminal and the old city centre. Taxis and local buses are also available.

Lecce Bus Station (Autostazione Lecce)

Location: Near the city centre, making it convenient to go to the major attractions in Lecce.

Overview: Lecce, known as the "Florence of the South," is another significant bus hub in Puglia, serving both regional and national routes. The bus terminal is well supplied by a variety of transit operators, both long-distance and local.

Bus services:

• Regional buses link Lecce to adjacent towns, including Gallipoli, Otranto, and Brindisi.

• National Buses: Lecce provides routes to cities outside the area, including Naples and Rome.

• International Buses: Lecce has links to adjacent Greece and Albania.

How To Get To The City:

The station is about a 15-minute walk from Lecce's old centre. Taxis and buses are available for transportation to other sections of the city.

Brindisi Bus Station (Autostazione Brindisi).

Location: Near the heart of Brindisi and not far from the harbour.

Overview: As an important port city in Puglia, Brindisi has a well-established bus network that serves regional, national, and international destinations.

Bus services:

Brindisi has regular regional bus connections to adjacent towns, including Ostuni, Lecce, and Ceglie Messapica.

• National Buses: The station serves major cities in Italy, including Bari, Naples, and Rome.

• International bus services connect Brindisi to Greece and other Mediterranean locations.

How To Get To The City:

The bus terminal is about 10 minutes from the city centre. Local taxis, buses, and trams are available for convenient transportation.

Foggia Bus Station (Autostazione Foggia).

Location: In the northern area of Puglia, near the city centre.

Overview: Foggia, a significant city in northern Puglia, serves as a regional bus hub. The bus station links tourists to communities in the Gargano National Park and other southern Italian cities.

Bus services:

✓ Regional buses link Foggia to cities in northern Puglia, including Manfredonia and San Severo, as well as surrounding communities.

• National bus services connect major Italian cities, including Rome, Naples, and Bari.

Foggia has bus links to neighbouring countries like Albania.

How To Get To The City:

The station is close to the city centre, so you can stroll to the major attractions in Foggia. Taxis and buses are available for people heading farther into the city.

Bus Travel Tips in Puglia

● Ticket options:

Tickets for buses can be purchased at the station, online, or through mobile apps. Booking long-distance buses in advance is suggested, particularly during peak seasons.

• Regional bus tickets cost €5-€20, depending on distance and route.

• Longer bus rides often cost between €20 and €40, depending on city and service type.

• Travel times:

• Regional bus travel from Bari to Lecce takes around 2.5-3 hours.

• Regional bus travel time from Bari to Brindisi is around 1.5 hours.

• Long-distance bus travel from Bari to Rome takes around 6-7 hours.

• Long-distance bus travel from Bari to Milan takes around 10-12 hours.

• The bus journey from Lecce to Rome takes around 7-8 hours.

● Book tickets:

Tickets for both regional and national buses are available from major bus operators such as FlixBus, MarinoBus, and Itabus. These firms run contemporary, luxurious buses that provide facilities like Wi-Fi, air conditioning, and reclining seats.

• Convenience:

While buses are slower than trains, they provide direct links to smaller towns and places that may not be reached by rail. Additionally, buses are often more affordable, especially for budget-conscious travellers.

● Scenic journeys:

Travelling by bus in Puglia can be a scenic experience, especially along regional routes. While en route to their destination, passengers may enjoy stunning views of the countryside, olive orchards, vineyards, and coastline.

• Luggage:

Most buses allow for one carry-on and one checked bag. Before embarking on your trip, be sure to verify the luggage rules of the bus operator you've chosen.

Benefits of Traveling by Bus in Puglia

● Affordable: Bus travel is a cost-effective alternative to rail travel.

● Buses provide flexibility in routes and timetables, particularly for reaching outlying locations not served by railroads.

● Scenic Routes: Slower bus excursions provide magnificent vistas of the Italian countryside.

● Buses provide contemporary facilities like Wi-Fi, air conditioning, and adjustable seats, making them comparable to trains for shorter trips.

Travelling by bus is a quick and cost-effective method to get to and around Puglia, whether you're visiting from other parts of Italy or seeing local attractions. While buses may be slower than other forms of transportation, they provide a unique chance to observe the Italian countryside and shore while travelling to some of the region's most picturesque places.

Getting to Puglia by Car

Driving to Puglia by automobile is a fantastic opportunity to see the area at your speed. With its gorgeous landscapes, coastal highways, and quaint villages, driving by automobile enables you to appreciate Puglia's beauty and flexibility while exploring rural locations that may be tougher to reach by public transit. Whether you're travelling from another area of Italy or overseas, renting a vehicle gives flexibility and ease for traversing the region's winding roads and scenic scenery.

Driving to Puglia from Major Italian Cities

• Bari (from Rome):

• Distance: Around 430 kilometers (267 miles).

• Driving time: around 4.5-5 hours.

• From Rome, take the A14 route south towards Bari. This straightforward route will take you through the gorgeous landscapes of Lazio and Apulia.

● Bari (via Naples):

• Distance: Around 250 kilometers (155 miles).

• Driving time: around 3–3.5 hours.

• Head southeast on the A16 highway towards Bari. The route winds through the hills of Campania and Apulia, with breathtaking vistas.

● Lecce (via Bari):

• Distance: Around 150 kilometers (93 miles).

• Driving time: around 1.5-2 hours.

• Travel south on the SS16 road, passing through picturesque coastal towns like Monopoli and Ostuni. This route allows you to visit some of Puglia's most iconic towns along the way.

• Lecce (from Rome):

• Distance: Around 600 kilometers (373 miles).

• Driving time: approximately 6.5-7 hours.

• Take the A1 highway south to Naples, then the A16 highway towards Bari. From Bari, take the SS16 highway to Lecce.

Driving in Puglia.

● Road conditions:

Puglia's roads are generally in good condition, particularly highways and major routes. The Autostrada (A14) and other major roads are well-kept and easy to travel on. In more remote areas, rural or coastal roads may be narrow, winding, or unpaved. Always drive carefully, especially in hilltop towns and on winding coastal routes.

● Traffic and Parking:

• Traffic: Major cities like Bari and Lecce may have congested traffic, particularly during the high tourist season (summer months). It's wise to arrange your trip to avoid city centres during peak hours.

• Parking: Parking in major cities may be problematic, especially in historic areas. Look for authorized parking places or park outside the city centre and utilize public transit to get to your location. In smaller places, parking is frequently simpler to locate.

● ZTL Zones:

Like many Italian cities, Bari, Lecce, and other ancient towns have limited traffic zones (Zona a Traffico Limitato, ZTL). Be aware of these zones, since driving or parking in certain places without authorization might result in penalties. ZTL zones are typically plainly designated, and it's essential to verify local restrictions before entering.

● Toll Roads:

Some highways in Puglia, such as the A14, are toll roads. The tolls may be paid at toll booths or via electronic devices (telepass) for speedier transit. Keep adequate cash or a credit card available while utilizing toll roads.

Advantages of Driving in Puglia

● Flexibility and freedom:

Renting a vehicle allows you to drive at your speed, visit local villages, and discover hidden treasures along the route. You can easily go to isolated regions like the Gargano National Park, the Itria Valley, and more.

● Scenic Drives:

Puglia has some of Italy's most attractive driving routes, including coastal roads with stunning views of the Adriatic Sea, olive orchards, vineyards, and picturesque hilltop towns. Driving through cities such as Alberobello, Polignano a Mare, and Matera allows you to appreciate the region's scenic splendour.

● Access to remote destinations:

Many of Puglia's most beautiful villages and beaches are off the beaten path and difficult to reach by public transportation. A vehicle makes it simpler to go to isolated locations such as the magnificent beaches of Salento or the picturesque rural towns of the Valle d'Itria.

Rental cars in Puglia

● Where to Rent?

Rental automobiles are commonly available at airports (e.g., Bari Karol Wojtyła Airport, Brindisi Airport) and large cities. There are international and local vehicle rental businesses such as Europcar, Hertz, Avis, and Sixt, as well as local ones. It is preferable to book in advance, particularly during high seasons.

● Cost:

Car rental prices vary according to the season, car type, and rental term. On average, a normal economy automobile will cost between €30 and €60 per day, with rates climbing throughout the summer. Remember to add in the cost of gasoline, tolls, and insurance.

• Requirements:

You must have a valid driver's license (an International Driving Permit is advised for non-EU tourists), a credit card, and be at least 21 years old.

Cost of Driving to Puglia

● Fuel:

Gas in Italy is quite costly. Expect to spend between €1.60 and €1.80 per litre for fuel or diesel. Make careful you fill up in major towns where costs are often cheaper.

• Tolls:

Tolls on roads such as the A14 may vary between €5 and €20, depending on the distance travelled. For example, the journey from Bari to Lecce costs around €10.

● Parking:

In major cities, parking prices may vary between €1 and €3 per hour. Check for free parking spots or park in approved lots, which might cost anything from €5 to €10 per day.

Tips for Driving in Puglia

• Navigation:

While Google Maps and other navigation applications are useful, it's always a good idea to have a paper map or GPS as a backup, particularly in rural regions where connections may be poor.

● Keep an eye out for cyclists and pedestrians:

Be wary of bicycles and pedestrians in towns and on smaller roads, particularly during the summer months when tourism is at its highest.

• Cultural Etiquette: Italians drive assertively, so expect speedier lane changes, particularly in cities. Always yield to pedestrians at crosswalks and adhere to local driving conventions.

Driving to Puglia is a rewarding experience that enables you to see the region's gorgeous scenery, quaint villages, and lovely coasts on your own time. Renting a vehicle may improve your vacation by allowing you to discover Puglia's hidden wonders with little planning and awareness of local driving conditions. Whether you're driving from a nearby city in Italy or visiting Puglia from overseas, this method of transportation provides flexibility, scenic splendour, and a real, immersive travel experience.

Chapter 4: Getting Around

Transportation Options

Transportation Options in Puglia.

Puglia, a compelling area in southern Italy, is well-connected by a variety of transportation choices, enabling travellers to easily move between its dynamic cities, stunning countryside, and picturesque villages. Whether you're visiting the beaches of Salento, the ancient capitals of Lecce and Bari, or the rolling hills of the Itria Valley, Puglia has various convenient transportation options to suit your needs and schedule.

Public Transportation

Puglia's public transit is rather efficient, particularly in major cities and villages, making it a useful alternative for those who want to explore without a vehicle. Here's a summary of the major public transportation options:

Buses

• Regional Bus Service:

Various firms run Puglia's regional bus network, the most famous of which are Ferrovie del Sud Est (FSE) and Sita Sud. These buses link the region's main cities and towns, including Bari, Lecce, Brindisi, Alberobello, and Polignano a Mare, as well as rural locations.

● Ticketing and Fares:

Bus tickets are often reasonably priced and may be bought at stations, newsstands, or straight from the driver. Fares typically vary from €1.50 and €3.00, depending on the route. Long-distance tickets might cost between €5 and €10.

● Schedule & Frequency:

Bus timetables vary by location and season, with more regular service during peak tourist season (spring to autumn). It's best to verify schedules online or at local bus stops, since some remote routes may only run a few times each day.

Trains

● Regional and intercity trains:

Trenitalia, Italy's national train service, provides the bulk of rail links in Puglia, including high-speed trains (Frecciarossa and Frecciabianca) that connect important towns like Bari, Lecce, and Brindisi. Ferrovie del Sud Est (FSE) provides a regional rail service that connects smaller towns, including rural and hilltop settlements.

● Main routes and travel times:

• The train ride from Bari to Lecce takes around 2-2.5 hours.

• Travel time by rail from Bari to Brindisi is around one hour.

• The travel time from Bari to Matera is around 1.5-2 hours.

• Travel time from Lecce to Ostuni is around 30-40 minutes.

● Ticket prices:

Train tickets are relatively inexpensive, ranging from €10 to €25 depending on the route, kind of train (local or high-speed), and level of service. Booking ahead of time allows you to get reduced tickets.

• Advantages:

Trains provide pleasant, rapid, and efficient long-distance transport between Puglia's main cities. Puglia's rail terminals are conveniently positioned, with regular and dependable service to and from towns like Bari, Lecce, and Brindisi.

Tram

● Tram Services for Cities:

Tram services are offered in certain places, especially Bari. Bari has a modest but effective tram network that runs across the city and links neighbourhoods such as Poggiofranco and Bari Vecchia (the old town).

● Ticket and Cost:

Tram tickets in Bari usually cost roughly €1.50 for a single travel. Tourists may also purchase unlimited travel passes, which provide access to the city's trams, buses, and local trains.

Car Rentals

Renting a vehicle is an excellent method to see Puglia, particularly if you want to visit rural villages or lovely coastal locations. The region's villages and cities are well linked by roadways, and driving allows you to explore at your speed.

● Where to Rent?

Rental automobiles are available at major airports like Bari Karol Wojtyła Airport, Brindisi Airport, and Lecce Railway Station. International automobile rental businesses like Hertz, Avis, and Europcar, as well as local ones, present a diverse selection of alternatives.

● Cost of renting a car:

A rental vehicle in Puglia typically costs between €30 and €60 per day for an economy automobile. Prices vary according to the season, automobile type, and rental period.

● Road conditions:

The roads of Puglia are typically in decent shape, however, certain rural roads and twisting coastline routes may be tiny or poorly maintained. Driving in Puglia is simple, with clear road signs; nevertheless, for the greatest experience, use a GPS or guidance program.

• Advantages:

Renting a vehicle offers considerable freedom, particularly for those who want to explore the countryside, visit smaller towns, or find off-the-beaten-path sites.

Taxis and Ridesharing

Taxis and ride-sharing services (like as Uber and Free Now) are widely accessible throughout Puglia's cities. They are especially beneficial for short journeys inside cities or to regions that are not readily accessible by public transportation.

Taxis

● Taxis are readily accessible in large cities like Bari, Lecce, and Brindisi, generally stationed in key locations such as rail stations or airports. You may also phone a cab or reserve one in advance via a local service.

● Taxi charges normally range from €3 to €5, with extra expenses for distance and duration.

Ride-Sharing

● Uber operates in major cities like Bari and Lecce, providing a handy alternative to conventional taxis.

● Cost: Ride-sharing services are often less expensive than taxis, particularly for short trips.

Bicycles and scooters

For the more adventurous visitor, renting a bike or scooter is a popular and environmentally responsible option to see Puglia, especially along the coast or in villages with small streets that are difficult to manage by automobile.

● Rental stores are accessible in most towns, particularly along the coast and in tourist destinations such as Polignano a Mare and Lecce. Many communities provide electric bike rentals for better access to difficult terrain.

● Bicycle rentals typically cost €15–€25 per day, while scooter rentals vary from €30–€50 per day depending on the kind.

● Renting a bike or scooter provides flexibility and an enjoyable way to explore Puglia's cities, beaches, and countryside. It's especially suitable for short journeys inside cities or beautiful roads.

Boats and Ferries

Puglia is famed for its stunning coastline, and going by boat or ferry is a wonderful opportunity to see the area from a fresh viewpoint. Ferries link Puglia to the rest of Italy and the Adriatic Sea islands.

• Ferries:

There are ferry services between Bari and Dubrovnik, Croatia. This path is particularly popular throughout the summer months among tourists looking to visit the Adriatic area.

Ferries from Bari to Montenegro leave many times every week.

● Boat Rental:

Renting a boat for the day or a few hours is an excellent way to get to know Puglia's coastal regions better. Many communities along the coast, notably Monopoli and Polignano a Mare, provide boat rentals.

Walking and Exploring by Foot

Puglia's towns are often best visited on foot, particularly the old cores of cities like Lecce, Bari, and Matera. Walking enables tourists to discover the beauty of small alleyways, gorgeous squares, and hidden jewels that might otherwise be overlooked while going by automobile or public transportation.

● Advantages of walking around Puglia's old towns include seeing local life, admiring architectural details, and experiencing the tranquil ambience of medieval settlements.

Puglia has a diverse range of transportation alternatives for guests, each tailored to particular interests and travel types. There are several methods to travel about, whether you use public transportation to go to main cities, hire a vehicle for more flexibility, or explore the area by bike, rail, or even boat. Depending on your schedule and the sites you want to visit, combining various forms of transportation might give you the most efficient and entertaining travel experience in Puglia.

Tips for navigating Puglia

Tips for navigating Puglia

Navigating through Puglia may be an interesting and rewarding experience, particularly given the attractive villages, picturesque landscapes, and coastline splendour. However, like with every location with its distinct features, there are a few pointers and methods that may help make your trip experience easier and more pleasurable. Here are some useful ideas to navigate Puglia:

Plan for seasonal variations.

● The peak tourist season in Puglia is from April to June and early fall (September to October). During these months, the weather is great, and the area isn't overcrowded.

● To avoid crowds, come during the off-season (November–March), albeit certain attractions may have restricted hours.

● Weather: Summers in Puglia may be scorching, particularly in inland locations like Matera and the Itria Valley. Always carry a drink, use sunscreen, and dress in lightweight clothes.

Prepare for Narrow Roads and Parking Challenges.

● Some communities, particularly in the Itria Valley and near the coast, feature narrow, twisting roads. If you're driving a rental automobile, be patient and cautious, especially while taking tight turns or going through alleys.

● Parking might be challenging, particularly in historical and tourist locations. Look for approved parking places and expect to pay a nominal price. In certain towns, you may have to park on the outskirts and walk into the centre.

Many Italian municipalities feature "Zona a Traffico Limitato" (ZTL) zones that limit access to certain areas to residents or authorized vehicles. To avoid penalties, be cautious of signage indicating ZTL zones. In these zones, only pedestrians or residents are permitted.

Use GPS and local maps.

● While GPS and navigation programs (e.g., Google Maps) are dependable, rural locations may have limited or obsolete information. It's a good idea to double-check instructions, particularly when visiting tiny towns or off-the-beaten-path sites.

● Local Maps: Tourist offices in old towns like Lecce, Bari, and Alberobello provide complimentary maps to assist visitors traverse tight alleys and identify significant attractions.

Learn basic Italian phrases.

● Language: While many people in Puglia understand basic English, particularly in tourist areas, learning a few Italian words might help make your vacation more pleasurable. Simple phrases include "Dove si trova···" (Where is...) and "Quanto costa?" (How much is it?) would be appreciated.

● Cultural Etiquette: Italians emphasize respectful communication. Always greet locals with "Buongiorno" (Good morning) or "Buona sera" (Good evening), and be courteous while interacting with them.

Be prepared for public transportation challenges.

● Bus and train timetables may vary, particularly in rural locations, notwithstanding their efficiency. Check schedules in advance, particularly for bus lines that run less often during the off-season.

● Validate your bus or rail ticket before boarding. Fines may be charged if your ticket is not stamped at the validation machine.

Accept the slow pace of life.

● Puglia is known for its laid-back atmosphere and slower pace of life. Take your time enjoying leisurely dinners, exploring little villages on foot, and taking in the scenery. Puglia is not a place to hustle; it is best enjoyed at a leisurely pace.

● Afternoon Siesta: Smaller communities may shut stores and restaurants between 1:00 PM and 4:00 PM for their afternoon break. Plan your touring and shopping appropriately.

Be mindful of rural villages and little amenities.

● Rural Areas: Although Puglia has beautiful rural towns and off-the-beaten-path attractions, services may be restricted during off-peak seasons. When going to more distant places, bring food, drink, and a charged phone.

● Smaller establishments, rural locations, and local markets may prefer cash payments over credit cards, however, most bigger cities allow them. Carry a small number of euros with you for these occasions.

Respect the local traditions and customs.

● Dress modestly while visiting religious locations, including churches. Shoulders and knees should be covered, notably in the Basilica di San Nicola in Bari and the Lecce Baroque churches.

● Dining Etiquette: Italians like casual dinners. Don't hurry through a dinner; it's an opportunity for discussion and pleasure. When eating out, it is usual to offer a little tip (between 5 and 10%) for excellent service, although tipping is not required.

Use travel apps for attractions and dining.

● Apps such as Tripadvisor, Google Maps, and local tourist apps may provide information on popular attractions, opening hours, and reviews. Many Puglia attractions have apps that provide information about historical buildings, restaurants, and activities.

● Food aficionados may use apps like TheFork (also known as Quandoo in Italy) and Yelp to book reservations and find the finest eateries in their neighbourhood.

Pack for the Region's Terrain.

● Footwear: Puglia is famed for its medieval villages with cobblestone walkways and hiking paths in natural areas like Gargano National Park. Walking through historic cities and seeing natural places requires comfortable, durable footwear.

● Sun Protection: The southern Italian sun may be harsh, particularly in summer. Pack sunscreen, sunglasses, and a hat to keep yourself safe while exploring.

Navigating Puglia may be a lovely experience if you're prepared and aware of the region's distinct features. Whether you're using public transit, renting a vehicle, or exploring on foot, these recommendations will help you have a seamless and stress-free trip to this gorgeous region of Italy. Take your time, appreciate the local culture, and enjoy Puglia's breathtaking scenery and rich history.

Chapter 5: Cuisines to Try

Signature dishes.

Signature dishes of Puglia

Orecchiette pasta.

● Ingredients: Orecchiette, or "little ears" in Italian, are prepared of durum wheat semolina and water. The dough is flattened into little discs that resemble ears. The pasta is often served with a variety of sauces, the most popular of which include broccoli rabe, anchovies, garlic, and chilli flakes.

● Where to Get Them: Orecchiette may be found at restaurants across Puglia, particularly in Bari, Lecce, and Matera. Local shops and grocery stores sell fresh or dried orecchiette.

● The cost of orecchiette pasta in restaurants varies from €8 to €15, depending on the sauce and institution. Markets sell dried orecchiette at roughly €2−€5 for every 500g box.

Focaccia Barese

Ingredients: Focaccia Barese is a thick, fluffy flatbread topped with cherry tomatoes, olives, and a liberal drizzle of olive oil. The dough is created with wheat, yeast, water, and olive oil, resulting in a delicate texture. It's seasoned with rosemary, sea salt, and sometimes garlic.

Focaccia Barese is widely available at bakeries and pizzerias in Bari and adjacent cities. It's a popular street meal, so you'll see it at many cafés and marketplaces.

● Cost: A slice of Focaccia Barese ranges from €2 to €5, depending on size and location. Whole focaccia breads may cost €5 to €8.

Panzerotti

● Panzerotti are miniature, deep-fried turnovers stuffed with various fillings. The most typical fillings are tomato and mozzarella, although versions with ham, ricotta, and even more inventive ingredients like mushrooms or spinach are available. The dough is created with wheat, yeast, and olive oil.

● Panzerotti may be found at pizzerias, street food vendors, and bakeries across Puglia, including the popular Panzerotti Di Lella in Bari. Many other places have local variants of this meal.

● A panzerotto may cost between €2.50 and €4, depending on size and contents. Some restaurants may provide bigger servings for between €5 and €8.

Bombette

● Ingredients: Bombettes are tiny skewered meat buns cooked with pig or beef, packed with cheese (usually caciocavallo), and seasoned with herbs and spices like garlic, salt, and pepper. They are then grilled or roasted over an open flame, resulting in a juicy and tasty meal.

● Bombettes are often found in the Murgia area, namely in Cisternino and Alberobello. These towns are well-known for their butchers and traditional cafés that serve grilled bombette.

● Cost: Bombette may be ordered as part of a mixed grill platter at local restaurants for about €10 to €15. When bought separately, bombettes generally cost between €2 and €3.

These characteristic dishes are part of Puglia's rich culinary tradition, and sampling them is a must during any visit to the province. From the simple beauty of orecchiette pasta to the decadent, deep-fried richness of panzerotti, each dish represents a distinct flavour of southern Italian cuisine. You may find them at local restaurants, street vendors, and marketplaces, with pricing varying depending on location and serving size.

Regional Snacks and Drinks.

Snacks and Drinks from Puglia

Taralli

Taralli is a crunchy, ring-shaped snack prepared with wheat, olive oil, white wine, and salt. They may be served simply or seasoned with fennel seeds, black pepper, or chile. After being fashioned into rings, they are gently boiled before baking to acquire their crunchy texture.

Taralli is a popular snack in Puglia, available in bakeries, markets, and street food vendors. They may be found in practically every town, and are often sold in huge, colourful bags at local stores.

● Taralli prices range from €3 to €6 per bag (250g to 500g), depending on where bought.

Fave e Cicoria

● Ingredients: Fave e Cicoria is a classic meal using broad beans (fave) and wild chicory (cicoria), a leafy green. The beans are often cooked to a creamy, stew-like consistency, and the cicoria is sautéed with garlic and olive oil. The cuisine is hearty and nutritious, highlighting the region's agricultural background.

Where to Get Them: This meal is a popular snack or side dish in rural Puglia, particularly in places like Altamura and Gravina di Puglia. It may be found in most local trattorias and restaurants, particularly those that serve traditional Pugliese cuisine.

● Fave e Cicoria is often served with dinner and costs between €7 and €12 per dish in restaurants. Local markets sell fresh broad beans and chicory for roughly €3 to €5 per kilo.

Pugliese olives.

● Ingredients: Pugliese olives are noted for their rich, briny taste, derived from the region's olive trees. The most popular types include Cellina di Nardò, Ogliarola Salentina, and Leccino olives. These olives are often seasoned with olive oil, garlic, oregano, and other spices.

Pugliese olives are available in grocery stores, marketplaces, and specialist food shops across Puglia. They are also available in local olive oil mills, where you may get them straight from the source.

● Marinated olives range in price from €4 to €8 per jar, depending on quality and quantity. You may purchase them loose at marketplaces for about €3 and €6 per kilo.

Frise

● Ingredients: Frise are typical Pugliese bread rings cooked twice for a crispy, dry texture. They are usually served with a variety of toppings, such as fresh tomatoes, olive oil, and sometimes garlic, oregano, or olives. Frise, which are often consumed as a snack or light meal, are ideally soaked in water to soften the texture before eating.

● Frise may be found at bakeries and small food stores in Puglia, particularly in coastal towns like Otranto and Gallipoli. They are often served with fresh ingredients like tomatoes and basil.

● Cost: Frise are often offered in packs of two or more, with costs ranging from €2 to €5 depending on the bakery and area.

These regional nibbles embody the tastes of Puglia's modest yet colourful cuisine. Whether it's the crisp bite of Taralli, the rustic heartiness of Fave e Cicoria, the tangy joy of Pugliese Olives, or the pleasing texture of Frise, each snack is a delectable sample of southern Italy's culinary traditions. They are ideal for eating on their own or as part of a bigger lunch while visiting the area.

Chapter 6. Best Restaurants

Fine dining.

Fine Dining Restaurants in Italy.

Osteria Francescana, Modena.

What To Expect:
● Led by Chef Massimo Bottura, this world-renowned restaurant has three Michelin stars.
● Our culinary adventure mixes classic Italian tastes with new methods and beautiful presentation.
● Signature dishes include the famous "Oops! I Dropped the Lemon Tart" and "Five Ages of Parmigiano Reggiano."
● The environment is stylish and cosy, with a mix of contemporary and traditional design.
Where To Find It:
● Location: Via Stella 22, 41121 Modena, Italy.
● Visitors to the Emilia-Romagna area may easily reach Modena either by rail or by vehicle.
Cost:
● Tasting meals vary from €320 to €400 per person, without wine pairings.
● Reservations must be made months in advance.

Piazza Duomo (Alba)

What To Expect:
● Three-Michelin-star experience with Chef Enrico Crippa's innovative Piedmontese cuisine.
● Fresh, locally sourced foods, including those from the restaurant's biodynamic garden.
● Known for its seasonal tasting menus including Alba's famed white truffles.
● Located in the centre of Alba, this location is both beautiful and modern.
Where To Find It:
● Location: Piazza Risorgimento 4, 12051 Alba CN, Italy.
● Alba, located in the Piedmont area, is a popular culinary and wine destination, particularly during truffle season.
Cost:
● Tasting meals cost from €250-€300 per person, with optional wine pairings available for an additional fee.
● Reservations are strongly suggested, especially during the fall truffle season.

La Pergola (Rome)

What To Expect:
● Chef Heinz Beck runs Rome's only three-Michelin-starred restaurant.
● A sumptuous dining experience combining Mediterranean and Italian cuisines with a modern touch.
● Signature meals include "Fagottelli Carbonara" and exquisite desserts.
● The Rome Cavalieri Hotel provides stunning views of the Eternal City from its rooftop.
Where To Find It:
● Location: Via Alberto Cadlolo, 101, 00136 Roma, Italy.
● Easily accessible by taxi or public transportation in Rome.
Cost:
● Tasting dinners cost €270–€350 per person, while the wine list includes wines ranging from €50 to above €10,000.
To reserve a table, please book ahead of time.

Restaurant Enrico Bartolini (Milan)

What To Expect:
● Located in the MUDEC (Museum of Cultures), this two-Michelin-star restaurant highlights Chef Enrico Bartolini's innovative Italian cuisine.
● Offers a combination of classic and avant-garde cuisine, with a focus on innovation and perfection.
● Notable dishes include the "Risotto with Beetroot and Gorgonzola Essence" and beautifully presented desserts.
● The elegant and modern atmosphere complements the museum's beautiful setting.
Where To Find It:
● Location: Via Tortona 56, 20144 Milan, Italy.
● Located in Milan's lively design zone, conveniently accessible by tram or subway.
Cost:
● Tasting meals cost €180–€250 per person.
Reservations are advised, especially during weekends and high travel seasons.
Each of these restaurants provides a distinct and exceptional eating experience, making them must-sees for gourmet visitors to Italy.

Local favourites

Local Favorite Restaurants in Puglia

Osteria Le Pignatte, Bari.

What To Expect:

● Local favourite serving authentic Apulian food in a pleasant, rustic environment.
● The restaurant specializes in handcrafted orecchiette pasta, fresh fish, and seasonal products from local markets.
● The warm and friendly ambience, along with attentive service, make it an ideal venue for real culinary experiences.

How to get there:
● Location: Via Nicola de Giosa in Bari, Italy.
● Easy access from the city centre by walking, public transportation, or a short taxi journey. Bari is easily accessible by plane, rail, and vehicle for visitors from various locations.

Cost:
● Meal prices typically vary from €25–€40 per person, depending on selected meals and beverages.

Antichi Sapori (Lecce).

What To Expect:
● A farm-to-table restaurant known for utilizing fresh, local, and organic foods.
● Chef Pietro Zito's cuisine combines traditional Puglian dishes with contemporary methods, like stuffed vegetables and slow-cooked beef.
● The rustic and quiet location has an outdoor sitting area surrounded by olive trees and a bright herb garden.

How to get there:
● Location: Via Speranza 47, Montegrosso, Lecce, Italy.
● Located in the countryside of Lecce, about a 20-minute drive from the city centre. A vehicle or cab is advised for simple transportation.

Cost:
● Our tasting menus and à la carte selections vary from €30 to €60 per person, providing excellent value for the quality.

La Tana del Lupo (Polignano a Mare)

What To Expect:
● A little restaurant in Polignano a Mare offers traditional Apulian cuisine with an emphasis on seafood.
● Signature dishes include grilled octopus, pasta with sea urchins, and tiramisu.
● The décor echoes the beauty of the seaside town, creating a comfortable and family-friendly atmosphere.

How to get there:
● Location: Via Roma in Polignano a Mare, Italy.
● Conveniently located in the town's historic core, close to popular attractions. Polignano a Mare is readily accessible by rail or vehicle from Bari and the surrounding cities.

Cost:

● The average lunch costs €20–€35 per person.

Ristorante Al Fornello da Ricci, Foggia

What To Expect:
● This Michelin-starred restaurant combines traditional and innovative Puglian food.
● Locally sourced ingredients are used to create specialities like handmade pasta, slow-cooked lamb, and inventive desserts.
● The environment is both beautiful and friendly, with an emphasis on offering a memorable dining experience.
How to get there:
● Location: Contrada Montevicoli 13, Ceglie Messapica, Foggia, Italy.
● Located in the countryside of Foggia, about 40 minutes by vehicle from the city centre. A vehicle or private transportation is strongly advised.
Cost:
● Tasting meals begin at €50 per person, with à la carte choices available. The restaurant is well-known for its exceptional wine pairings, which come at an additional fee.

These restaurants reflect the variety and depth of Puglia's culinary landscape, each providing a one-of-a-kind experience that mixes traditional dishes with great service.

Chapter 7. Accommodation Options

Luxury hotels in Puglia.

Borgo Egnazia (Fasano)

What To Expect:

● Borgo Egnazia, a luxury resort near Fasano, is built to imitate a typical Apulian hamlet. It mixes architectural beauty, contemporary luxury, and real local character.

● The resort's rooms, villas, and suites are elegantly constructed with natural materials and neutral tones for a calm setting.

● Guests may enjoy world-class facilities, including a private beach club, two championship golf courses, various pools, and a magnificent spa with Mediterranean-inspired treatments.

● Dining choices include fine dining and informal, with regional specialities made from locally produced ingredients. The main restaurant, Due Camini, offers a Michelin-starred culinary experience.

● Activities include culinary courses, wine tastings, bike tours, and visits to local historic towns, providing a great balance of rest and adventure.

How to get there:

● Location: Savelletri di Fasano, Puglia, Italy.

• The closest airports are Bari Karol Wojtyła Airport (about 50 minutes by car) and Brindisi Salento Airport (about 45 minutes by car).

● Fasano station is easily accessible by train from Bari and Brindisi, and the resort is just a 15-minute drive away.

● The resort is conveniently accessible via the SS379 highway. Guests may park for free.

Cost:

● Standard rooms start at €500 per night during low season, while suites and villas may cost up to €1,000 per night during peak season. Meals and spa services are billed individually. Borgo Egnazia is suitable for tourists seeking luxury and seclusion.

Palazzo Guglielmo, Gallipoli

What To Expect:

The Palazzo Guglielmo is a boutique hotel located in the picturesque town of Vignacastrisi near Gallipoli, housed in an 18th-century palace. It has a distinct combination of historical charm and contemporary comfort.

● The hotel offers magnificent rooms and suites with soaring ceilings, antique furniture, and contemporary conveniences. Many apartments have garden views, which adds to the quiet atmosphere.

The amenities include a courtyard with a swimming pool, jacuzzi, and library for peaceful leisure.

● Guests may enjoy traditional Puglian food in the on-site restaurant, or take part in olive oil tastings and cookery workshops.

● Located near Gallipoli and the Salento coastline, it is an ideal base for visiting neighbouring beaches, towns, and cultural attractions.

How to get there:

● Located at Vignacastrisi, near Gallipoli, Puglia, Italy.

● The closest airport is Brindisi Salento, which is about 1.5 hours away by vehicle. Bari Karol Wojtyła Airport is about 2.5 hours distant.

● Gallipoli Station is the nearest major rail station. From there, it is advisable to take a cab or hire a vehicle to the property.

● The hotel is easily accessible by car from Lecce and other Salento towns. Guests may park on-site.

Cost:

● Standard rooms start at about €150 per night, while suites may cost up to €300 during high seasons. Meals and other activities, such as cooking workshops, are paid separately.

● Palazzo Guglielmo provides an intimate and genuine Puglian experience in a tranquil rural location.

Borgo Egnazia and Palazzo Guglielmo provide exceptional accommodations, whether you want elegance and refinement or an intimate, culturally engaging retreat. Each house offers a glimpse of Puglia's enthralling character, making your vacation genuinely unforgettable.

Budget-friendly stays

B&B La Finestra Sul Mare (Polignano a Mare)

What To Expect:

● This beautiful bed-and-breakfast has spectacular sea views, a warm and friendly ambience, and a pleasant home-like setting. Located in the charming village of Polignano a Mare, it is suitable for budget-conscious guests who want to stay comfortable.

The rooms are modernly designed and equipped with facilities like air conditioning, Wi-Fi, and flat-screen TVs. Many accommodations have balconies that overlook the beautiful seas of the Adriatic.

● Enjoy a great breakfast with fresh local foods, including pastries, fruits, and coffee, while taking in stunning sea views.

● Guests may easily discover Polignano a Mare's medieval town, cliffside beaches, and the iconic Lama Monachile Bridge.

How to get there:

• By Air: Bari Karol Wojtyła Airport is around 40 minutes away by vehicle or cab.

● Train passengers may easily reach the hotel from Polignano a Mare station, which is only a short walk away.

● The property is easily accessible by car via the SS16 highway, with close parking.

Cost:

● Standard double rooms start at about €80 per night, making them an affordable option. Breakfast is usually included in the fee.

Highlights:

● B&B La Finestra sul Mare is ideal for couples and lone visitors seeking a budget-friendly stay in a prominent location. Its closeness to Polignano's main attractions makes it an ideal destination for touring.

Ostello Salento (Lecce).

What To Expect:

● Ostello Salento is a budget-friendly hostel in Lecce that provides a communal environment and is a great starting point for visiting Salento's attractions.

● The hostel offers clean and pleasant individual rooms and shared dorms, making it suitable for budget-conscious visitors, groups, and families.

● Common spaces include a kitchen, lounge, and outdoor patio, creating a community-oriented atmosphere.

The hostel offers activities such as local excursions, cultural experiences, and culinary courses to engage visitors in the region's culture.

● The location is excellent for experiencing Lecce's Baroque architecture, historical monuments, and lively nightlife. Beaches on the Adriatic and Ionian shores are readily accessible from here.

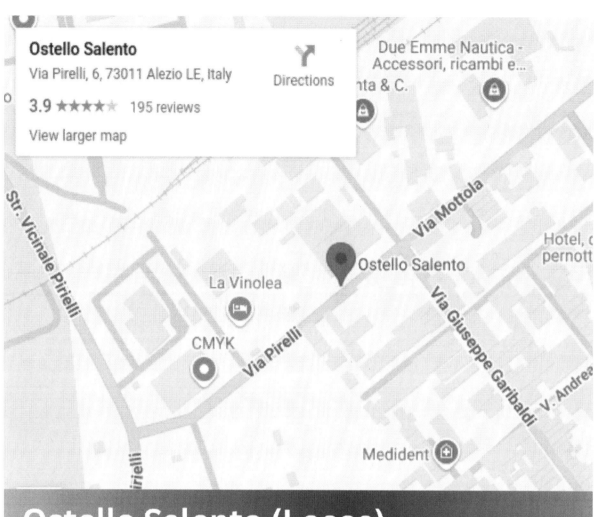

Ostello Salento (Lecce)

SCAN THE QR CODE

1. Open your device's camera app.
2. Align the QR code within the camera frame.
3. Wait for the code to be recognized.
4. Check the displayed notification or link.
5. Tap to access the linked content or information.

How to get there:

● The nearest airport is Brindisi Salento, which is around 45 minutes away by car or bus.

● The major train station in Lecce is a 15-minute walk or short taxi ride away from the hostel.

● Access the hostel by car via the SS613 highway. There is little on-street parking accessible nearby.

Cost:

● Dormitory beds start at €25 per night, while private rooms cost between €50 and €70. This covers necessities and access to common areas.

Highlights:

● Ostello Salento is ideal for budget-conscious guests seeking a welcoming and energetic atmosphere. Its mix of low cost, cultural events, and central position make it an excellent alternative for visiting Lecce and beyond.

Both lodgings have distinct advantages: B&B La Finestra sul Mare offers a tranquil escape with breathtaking sea views, whilst Ostello Salento appeals to social visitors seeking affordability and cultural immersion in Lecce. Each promises an unforgettable vacation in Puglia.

Unique Experiences

Unique Accommodation Experiences in Puglia.

Masseria San Domenico (Savelletri).

What To Expect:

● Masseria San Domenico is a magnificent five-star resort in a beautifully renovated 15th-century Masseria (farmhouse) surrounded by olive orchards on the Adriatic coast. It's an ideal combination of historical charm and contemporary luxury.

The resort's beautiful rooms and suites have typical Puglian characteristics such as whitewashed walls, wooden beams, and antique furniture. The rooms provide contemporary conveniences like Wi-Fi, flat-screen TVs, and marble baths.

The resort offers a variety of amenities, including a thalassotherapy treatment, an outdoor pool, and a private beach club with direct access to the Adriatic Sea.

● The on-site restaurant offers delicious Mediterranean cuisine using locally sourced products, including olive oil grown on the estate. A handpicked wine list includes some of the best local and international options.

● Activities include culinary courses, wine tasting, cycling through olive fields, and guided trips to adjacent medieval villages like Fasano and Alberobello.

How to get there:

• By Air: Brindisi Salento Airport is about 50 minutes distant by vehicle. Bari Karol Wojtyła Airport is around an hour and 15 minutes distant.

● Fasano Train Station is about 15 minutes by vehicle from the property. Private transport may be provided on request.

● Located off the SS379 highway, the Masseria provides free parking to customers.

Cost:

● Room rates start at about €450 per night, varying by season and room type. The fee includes breakfast, entrance to the pool, and usage of the beach club. Spa treatments and other activities may entail extra fees.

Significance:

● Masseria San Domenico is a top-tier resort for guests seeking a nice and relaxing getaway. Its focus on health, great eating, and cultural events sets it apart in Puglia.

Hotel La Peschiera (Monopoli

What To Expect:

● Hotel La Peschiera is an exceptional boutique hotel on the Adriatic coast that provides a calm and private vacation. With a small number of rooms, it ensures privacy and customized care.

● The hotel's rooms and suites are stylishly furnished in a minimalist Mediterranean style, with neutral tones, natural materials, and huge windows providing uninterrupted sea views. Each accommodation has direct access to one of the hotel's pools or the private beach.

The property has seven linked seawater pools, a private beach area, and a waterfront patio for leisure.

● The on-site gourmet restaurant offers fresh seafood and traditional Puglian meals, along with a great range of area wines. Dining outside with views of the Adriatic is a delight.

● Activities include yoga, boat tours, and seeing neighbouring sights like Monopoli's historic core and Alberobello's unique trulli dwellings.

How to get there:

● By Air: Brindisi Salento Airport is around 50 minutes by vehicle, while Bari Karol Wojtyła Airport is about 1 hour away.

● The Monopoli Train Station is a 15-minute drive from the hotel. Transfers may be performed upon request.

● Access the hotel by car via the SS16 highway. Guests may park on-site.

Cost:

● Room rates start from €500 per night, including breakfast. Additional services, such as spa treatments or private trips, may incur additional fees.

Significance:

● Hotel La Peschiera offers a luxury and intimate beachside hideaway. Its prime location, facilities, and superb cuisine make it one of Monopoli's most sought-after lodgings.

Masseria San Domenico and Hotel La Peschiera are the epitomes of Puglian luxury, providing one-of-a-kind experiences that blend stunning scenery, superb service, and real Puglian charm. Whether you like the ancient atmosphere of a Masseria or the tranquillity of a coastal resort, these lodgings will provide an enjoyable stay.

Chapter 8: Festivals and Events

Seasonal celebrations

Seasonal Celebrations in Puglia

La Festa di San Nicola (Bari

What To Expect:
● La Festa di San Nicola is a prominent religious and cultural celebration in southern Italy, honouring St. Nicholas, Bari's patron saint. The celebration attracts pilgrims and guests from all around the world.

● The three-day festival in early May includes a procession of a statue of St. Nicholas through the streets and out to sea on a boat, representing his landing in Bari.

Highlights include religious masses, traditional music, local dance performances, fireworks, and an outdoor market with regional delicacies, crafts, and souvenirs.

● The ancient town of Bari is magnificently lighted, providing a wonderful ambience that merges spirituality and celebration.

When and Where?

● The festival takes place yearly from May 7 to May 9 in Bari, with major festivities taking place at the Basilica di San Nicola and along the seashore.

How to get there:

• By Air: Bari Karol Wojtyła Airport is easily accessible from major Italian and European cities. It is about 30 minutes by cab or shuttle from the city centre.

● The festival sites are a short walk from Bari Centrale Station, which is easily accessible by Italy's major rail lines.

● The A14 highway provides easy access to Bari by car. Parking may be restricted at the event, so plan appropriately.

Cost:

● Free entry to the event. However, some activities, such as food and souvenirs or guided tours, may incur extra fees.

Festa di San Vito (Polignano a Mare).

What To Expect:

● The Festa di San Vito is a spectacular event honouring the patron saint of Polignano a Mare.

Highlights include a religious procession with a statue of San Vito, live folk music, traditional dances, and a big market.

● The celebration is known for its stunning fireworks display that illuminates the cliffs and water. During the event, visitors may sample local delights like as fresh fish and homemade gelato.

When and Where?

● Held annually on June 15 in Polignano a Mare, the festival features activities across the town, particularly in the historic core and seaside districts.

How to get there:

Polignano a Mare has a rail station that connects to Bari and Lecce. The station is located within walking distance of the town centre.

● Polignano a Mare is a 40-minute drive from Bari via the SS16 highway.

• The closest airport is Bari Karol Wojtyła, which is around a 45-minute drive away.

Cost:

• Attendance is free. Food, drink, and souvenirs bought during the celebration may incur additional costs.

Taranta Festival (Melpignano

What To Expect:

● The Taranta Festival highlights Puglia's traditional folk music and dance, particularly the captivating pizzica dance. It's a cultural feast that combines history, music, and entertainment.

The event includes performances by local and foreign performers, seminars on pizzica dance, and cultural displays. It culminates with the concerto, a massive final concert attended by thousands.

● Visitors may enjoy the vibrant environment, and regional foods, and visit Melpignano, a lovely village.

When and Where?

● The August celebration covers numerous villages in Salento, with the major event being in Melpignano on the final Saturday of the month.

How to get there:

● Train: The closest major station is Lecce. From there, shuttle buses go to Melpignano.

● Melpignano is a 30-minute drive from Lecce, accessible via local roads.

● The nearest airport is Brindisi Salento Airport, which is about an hour's drive from Melpignano.

Cost:

● While general entrance is free, VIP seating and guided festival experiences may incur extra fees.

Night of Taranta (Salento)

What To Expect:

● La Notte della Taranta is a major music event in Italy that honours the traditional pizzica music of Puglia.

● The festival features local pizzica players, foreign performers, and orchestras, blending traditional and modern music.

In addition to music, the festival has food booths, artisan markets, and cultural programs to immerse visitors in Puglia's traditions.

When and Where?

● The festival takes place yearly in August, featuring performances in several towns in Salento. The major event takes place in Melpignano, drawing tens of thousands of fans.

How to get there:

● Train: Arrive in Lecce, then take a shuttle or drive to Melpignano.

Melpignano is conveniently accessible by vehicle and offers parking for event participants.

● Air: The nearest airport is Brindisi Salento Airport, which is about an hour away.

Cost:

● Entry is usually free, although fees for food, beverages, and souvenirs may apply.

Significance

These events commemorate Puglia's rich culture, history, and customs, providing tourists with unique experiences. From religious rites to exuberant music and dancing, these events provide a glimpse into Puglia's character and are a must-see for everyone visiting the province.

Cultural Highlights in Puglia

Puglia, a region rich in history and traditions, is a treasure trove of cultural highlights. From its ancient architecture and religious landmarks to its vibrant festivals and unique culinary experiences, Puglia offers visitors a glimpse into Italy's past and present. Here's an exhaustive look at the cultural gems you can explore in this enchanting region.

Historic and Religious Sites

The Trulli of Alberobello

- These iconic cone-shaped stone houses, a UNESCO World Heritage site, are an architectural marvel. The Trulli, built without mortar, are a testament to the ancient building techniques of the Itria Valley.
- **Explore:** Wander through the historic districts of **Rione Monti** and **Rione Aia Piccola**, where these traditional houses line the streets, and visit the **Trullo Sovrano**, the largest and most famous trullo.

Castel del Monte

- A striking octagonal fortress built by the Holy Roman Emperor **Frederick II** in the 13th century. Its unusual geometry and alignment with celestial bodies make it a fascinating site.
- **What to see:** The castle's geometric precision, its perfectly symmetrical design, and the panoramic views of the surrounding countryside.

Basilica di San Nicola in Bari

- This Romanesque church in the heart of **Bari** is dedicated to Saint Nicholas, whose relics are housed here. It is one of the most significant pilgrimage sites for Christians.
- **Explore:** The crypt where Saint Nicholas' relics are kept, the magnificent mosaics, and the impressive Romanesque façade.

The Roman Amphitheater of Lecce

- Situated in the historic center of **Lecce**, this Roman amphitheater dates back to the 2nd century and once hosted gladiatorial combat and theatrical performances.
- **What to see:** The preserved seating, arena, and surrounding Roman ruins, as well as the nearby **Piazza Sant'Oronzo**, where the amphitheater is located.

Matera's Sassi District

- **Matera**, a UNESCO World Heritage site, is known for its ancient cave dwellings carved into limestone hillsides. This prehistoric settlement, one of the world's oldest, has been continuously inhabited for thousands of years.

- **Explore:** Wander through the **Sassi di Matera**, visit ancient cave churches with frescoes, and learn about the town's fascinating history as you explore its winding streets.

Festivals and Traditions

La Taranta Festival

- The **La Notte della Taranta** is the largest festival dedicated to the traditional **Pizzica** dance and music, held annually in the **Salento** region. The festival celebrates Puglia's folkloric traditions, with performances by local musicians, dancers, and artists.
- **What to expect:** A vibrant atmosphere with lively folk music, dancers dressed in traditional costumes, and celebrations in towns like **Melpignano** and **Corigliano d'Otranto**.
- **Festa di San Nicola in Bari**

This religious festival, held in May, honors Saint Nicholas, the patron saint of Bari. Pilgrims from around the world come to participate in the feast, which includes a procession, music, and vibrant celebrations.
- **What to expect:** A grand procession through the streets of Bari, with hundreds of people following the saint's relics, accompanied by music, fireworks, and traditional food.

Feast of the Madonna della Madia in Monopoli

- This celebration in the town of **Monopoli** honors the arrival of the Madonna della Madia, the town's patron saint. The event, which takes place in early December, is marked by a lively procession, fireworks, and traditional Puglian music.
- **What to expect:** The procession of the Madonna, local bands playing traditional music, and the vibrant atmosphere of the town as people gather in the streets.

Gargano Wild Festival

- Celebrating the region's natural beauty, culture, and traditions, this festival in the **Gargano** National Park blends music, art, and gastronomy.
- **What to expect:** Open-air concerts, art exhibitions, and local food tastings, all surrounded by the stunning natural landscapes of Gargano.

Carnevale di Putignano

- One of the oldest and most famous carnivals in Italy, the **Carnevale di Putignano** in **Putignano** is an exuberant celebration held annually in January and February.
- **What to expect:** Grand parades featuring elaborate masks, costumes, and floats, street performances, and a festive atmosphere in the charming town of Putignano.

Traditional Crafts and Artisanal Products

Ceramics from Grottaglie

- The town of **Grottaglie** is renowned for its ceramic craftsmanship, with an artisan tradition that dates back centuries. The town's historic center is dotted with workshops where you can watch artisans at work and purchase beautiful handcrafted ceramics.

- **What to explore:** Visit the **Ceramics Museum** in Grottaglie, wander through the **quartiere delle ceramiche**, and take home unique pieces of pottery, ranging from rustic to contemporary designs.

Olive Oil Production

- Puglia is Italy's largest producer of olive oil, and the region's ancient olive groves are integral to its agricultural culture.
- **What to see:** Visit local **olive oil mills**, participate in tastings, and learn about the traditional methods of pressing olives, which have been passed down for generations.
- **Notable towns: Andria**, **Altamura**, and **Bitonto** are famous for their high-quality olive oil.

Lace-Making in Canosa di Puglia

- Canosa di Puglia, a town rich in history, is also famous for its **macramé lace-making** tradition. Skilled artisans continue to craft delicate lace items using intricate techniques passed down through generations.
- **What to explore:** Visit local workshops to see lace-makers at work and purchase handmade lace items, including tablecloths, napkins, and delicate shawls.

Culinary Traditions

Orecchiette and Pasta Tradition

- One of the most famous traditional dishes in Puglia is **orecchiette**, a small, ear-shaped pasta typically served with **cime di rapa** (turnip tops) or tomato sauce and meatballs.
- **What to explore:** Take a cooking class to learn how to make orecchiette from scratch or visit local eateries where the dish is a staple of the menu.

Focaccia Barese

- A popular street food from **Bari**, **focaccia barese** is a delicious flatbread topped with tomatoes, olives, and a drizzle of olive oil.
- **What to explore:** Visit the bakeries of Bari to taste this savory treat, often paired with a glass of local wine.

Cucina di Mare (Seafood Cuisine)

- Given its long coastline, Puglia's cuisine heavily features seafood. Fresh fish, octopus, mussels, and cuttlefish are common ingredients in local dishes.
- **What to explore:** Try seafood dishes like **frittura di pesce** (fried fish), **cozze alla tarantina** (mussels cooked in a spicy tomato sauce), and **insalata di mare** (seafood salad).

Primitivo Wine and Local Vineyards

- Puglia is home to several indigenous grape varieties, with **Primitivo** being one of the most famous. The region's sunny climate and fertile soil provide ideal conditions for wine production.
- **What to explore:** Visit vineyards in the **Salento** area for wine tastings and tours, learning about the region's winemaking traditions and the unique characteristics of **Primitivo** and other Puglian wines.

Puglia's Unique Architecture

Baroque Architecture in Lecce

- Lecce is known as the "Florence of the South" for its remarkable Baroque architecture. The city is dotted with churches, palaces, and buildings adorned with intricate Baroque facades.
- **What to explore:** Visit the **Basilica di Santa Croce**, the **Piazza del Duomo**, and the **Church of San Matteo** to admire the ornate, flourished designs of Lecce's Baroque buildings.

The Norman-Swabian Castle in Bari

- Built by the Normans and later expanded by the Swabians, this castle in **Bari** stands as a powerful reminder of the region's medieval past.
- **What to explore:** Explore the castle's imposing structure, visit the museum housed within, and take in the views over the old town and the Adriatic Sea.

Natural and Cultural Landscape

Gargano National Park

- Located in the northern part of Puglia, the **Gargano National Park** is a natural haven with dense forests, dramatic cliffs, and coastal villages.
- **What to explore:** Visit the **Monte Sant'Angelo**, known for its pilgrimage site and medieval charm, and explore the ancient forests, limestone caves, and pristine beaches of the park.

The Itria Valley and Trulli

- The **Itria Valley**, dotted with **trulli** houses, is a UNESCO World Heritage Site. It is a

unique cultural landscape shaped by centuries of human habitation and agricultural practices.

- **What to explore:** Wander through the hilltop towns of **Locorotondo** and **Cisternino**, both offering panoramic views of the valley and showcasing traditional whitewashed architecture.

Puglia is a region of diverse cultural treasures, offering everything from medieval castles and ancient trulli to vibrant festivals, delicious cuisine, and a rich craft heritage. Each town and village has its own distinctive traditions and stories, making Puglia an unmissable destination for anyone seeking to experience Italy's authentic cultural richness.

Chapter 9. Travel Tips

Best time to visit Puglia

Puglia, with its beautiful coastline, lovely villages, and rich history, is a year-round attraction. However, the optimum time to come is determined by your weather, activity interests, and desired experience.

Spring (April through June)

● Pros:
• Spring's warm weather (15-25°C / 59-77°F) makes it perfect for outdoor activities, sightseeing, and visiting beaches without the summer crowds.
• Puglia has fewer tourists, allowing you a more relaxing experience of its sights and cities.
• Nature enthusiasts and photographers will like the countryside's rich and blooming landscapes.
● Cons:
The Adriatic and Ionian Seas may still be too chilly for swimming, particularly in April and May.
• Limited Festivals: Although there are some small festivals, Puglia's main summer festivities have not yet begun.

Summer (July–August)

● Pros:

• Summer weather is great for beach enthusiasts, with temperatures reaching 30°C (86°F) or more.

Summer is peak festival season, with events such as La Notte della Taranta and Festa di San Vito taking place around the area.

• Longer daylight hours allow for more outdoor activities.

● Cons:

Summer is the peak season in Puglia, particularly in renowned sites like Alberobello, Polignano a Mare, and Otranto. Hotels and attractions might be overcrowded and pricey.

• High temperatures may be oppressive, particularly in inland places. It may also make sightseeing uncomfortable.

• High demand leads to higher prices for accommodations and flights.

Autumn (September through November)

● Pros:

The weather is ideal for touring and outdoor activities, with temperatures ranging from 18-27°C (64-81°F) compared to summer.

• Harvest Season: Visit vineyards and olive fields to sample fresh products during the autumn harvest.

• With fewer tourists, you may still enjoy the area without the summer bustle.

● Cons:

• Shorter days mean less time to explore during daylight hours.

• Cooler water temperatures, especially in October and November, might make swimming less pleasurable, notwithstanding pleasant weather.

Winter (December through February)

● Pros:

• Peaceful Atmosphere: Winter is the least congested season, offering a relaxing experience with fewer visitors. It's ideal for individuals who want a calm and serene vacation.

• Lower prices for hotels, flights, and other services, making it an affordable alternative for vacationers.

Christmas and New Year's festivities in Bari and Lecce include beautiful lights, decorations, and local customs, contributing to the region's particular character.

● Cons:

• Cold Weather: Average temperatures in inland regions range from 5-12°C (41-54°F). While coastal locations remain warmer, it may still be too chilly for beach activities.

• Limited Attractions: Some seasonal enterprises, such as beach clubs and open-air restaurants, may shut throughout the winter season. In addition, there are fewer activities and festivals than in previous seasons.

● The best seasons to visit Puglia are spring (April—June) and autumn (September—November), which provide pleasant weather, fewer people, and beautiful scenery.
For beach lovers, summer (July-August) is ideal, but expect crowds and increased expenses due to high temperatures.
● For a Quiet, Budget-Friendly Experience: Winter (December—February) provides calm and affordable pricing, but expect chilly weather and restricted outdoor activities.

Packing and Local Etiquette in Puglia.

Packing Tips for Puglia.

When preparing for a vacation to Puglia, keep the region's temperature, local culture, and planned activities in mind. Here's a guide on what to bring for each season and activity:

• Clothing:

• For spring and autumn, light layers are perfect. Pack a mix of light sweaters, long-sleeved shirts, and a lightweight jacket or coat for chilly nights. Cotton and linen are both comfortable and breathable, making them ideal for city exploration and outdoor activities.

• In summer, use lightweight, breathable clothes. Consider sundresses, shorts, t-shirts, and swimsuits. To protect yourself from the harsh sun, remember to bring a hat and sunglasses. Bring a light sweater or shawl in the evenings, since temperatures may drop somewhat.

• Coastal regions often get warm winters, although interior places might be colder. Pack a warm jacket, layers, and suitable walking shoes. If you travel to higher elevations or rural places, you may need to bring a scarf and gloves.

• Footwear:

To explore Puglia's cobblestone streets and cities such as Lecce, Alberobello, and Otranto, wear comfortable walking shoes or sneakers.

• Pack flip-flops or sandals for beach trips.

For exploring Gargano National Park and other natural reserves, it's recommended to wear sturdy shoes or hiking boots.

• Sun Protection:

• Puglia's summer sun may be strong. Pack sunscreen, SPF lip balm, sunglasses, and a hat to protect yourself from the sun's rays.

• Swimsuit:

When visiting Polignano a Mare or Monopoli beaches, remember to bring your swimwear. Even if you travel outside of the summer, the region's Mediterranean climate allows for swimming from late spring to early fall.

● Adapters and chargers:

To use your gadgets in Italy, pack an adaptor for Type C, F, or L plugs. Also, remember to bring chargers for your equipment, particularly if you intend on photographing Puglia's breathtaking scenery and architecture.

● Light Jacket or Layer:

Even in July, nights may be chilly, particularly along the coast or at higher elevations. Bring a lightweight jacket or sweater for the evening.

Local Etiquette in Puglia.

Puglia, with its rich history and relaxed attitude, has its own set of conventions and etiquette that assure polite and pleasurable encounters. Here are a few things to remember:

● Hello:

• A handshake is the most usual greeting, although when meeting friends or acquaintances, a cheek kiss (on both cheeks) is often shared. This is especially frequent in less formal contexts.

It's customary to greet people with "Buongiorno" (Good morning) or "Buonasera" (Good evening), particularly when entering stores or restaurants.

• Dress Code:

• Italians often dress formally, particularly in the evening or while attending church. While casual clothes are OK for daytime tourism, it is vital to dress modestly while visiting holy places.

For supper at a decent restaurant, locals like to dress up significantly, so consider wearing smart attire, even if the location is casual.

● Dining Etiquette:

• Punctuality: Italians normally appear on time for business meetings, but it's okay to be late for social engagements like dinner (10-15 minutes).

• Italians want to eat leisurely and enjoy the experience, so avoid hurrying through your meal. It is normal to share plates, and you may be given more wine or bread. Keep your hands on the table (but not your elbows), and avoid placing them in your lap.

• Tipping is not required in Italy but is appreciated for excellent service. It is normal to leave a little tip of 5-10% in restaurants or round up the amount. In cafés and informal restaurants, you may leave your change or just round up.

● Respect for local traditions.

Puglia has a strong religious culture, particularly in Bari and Matera. When visiting churches or religious places, dress modestly (cover your shoulders and knees) and respect any religious rites or services.

• When visiting old churches or chapels, observe respectful quiet, particularly during services or worship.

• Public behavior:

The Italians, particularly in the south, have a casual approach to time and personal space. It is usual for individuals to speak loudly in public places, and this is not considered rude. However, while chatting with natives, try to keep a courteous tone.

• Southern Italy is known for its late-night culture, particularly in seaside areas. Don't be surprised to find busy streets and vibrant cafés long after midnight, especially during the summer.

● Shopping etiquette:

• When entering a business, greet the owner or personnel with a cheerful "Buongiorno" or "Ciao." When completing a purchase, remember to say "Grazie" (thank you).

• Bargaining is more usual at marketplaces or while purchasing handcrafted items, like pottery, in villages like Grottaglie.

● Respect for nature:

Puglia has wonderful natural settings, including olive trees and beaches. Respect the environment by properly disposing of rubbish and according to any municipal conservation requirements.

Keeping these packing recommendations and local etiquette requirements in mind will ensure that you enjoy all Puglia has to offer while being respectful of its customs and traditions.

Chapter 10. Conclusion

Make the Most of Your Puglia Adventure

Puglia, with its rich history, magnificent coastline, wonderful food, and distinct culture, provides tourists with a wealth of fascinating experiences. There are various ways to make the most of your stay in this lovely southern Italian area, whether you're touring old cities, relaxing on gorgeous beaches, or eating local cuisine. Here's how to get the most out of your Puglia adventure:

Embrace the slow pace.

Puglia's appeal stems from its peaceful, easygoing lifestyle. While it's tempting to run around to see everything, take the time to sit down and appreciate the present moment. Allow yourself to absorb the moment, whether you're having a coffee in a picturesque town centre or meandering through the little alleyways of Otranto or Alberobello.

● Tip: Don't try to see everything in one visit. Instead, focus on a few important locations to fully immerse yourself in the local culture, people, and lifestyle.

Explore the lesser-known gems.

While well-known attractions like Alberobello's Trulli Houses, Castel del Monte, and Lecce's Baroque Churches are must-sees, Puglia is also rich with hidden gems that are sometimes ignored. Off the main road, see calmer towns, picturesque seaside villages, and pristine landscapes.

Explore Cisternino's ancient centre and tasty meat grills, Polignano a Mare's stunning cliffs and caves, and the Gargano National Park, ideal for nature lovers and hikers.

Spend time on the beach.

Puglia has some of Italy's most stunning beaches, particularly along the Adriatic and Ionian shores. Make sure to schedule some time for beach relaxation.

● Beaches to visit include Gallipoli for golden sand, Polignano a Mare for stunning cliffs and secret coves, and Torre Guaceto Nature Reserve for calm shoreline.

● Tip: Arrive early, particularly during warmer months, since beaches may get overcrowded. For a relaxing day, remember to bring sunscreen, a hat, and a towel.

Experience Puglia's Culinary Delights

One of the delights of visiting Puglia is its delectable food. Make the most of your vacation by sampling regional specialities whenever possible. There are many different cuisines to try, from fresh seafood to creative pasta dishes.

● Must-try dishes:

• Orecchiette pasta paired with turnip tops (cime di rapa).

• Bombettes are delicious meat buns stuffed with cheese and seasonings.

• Panzerotti are deep-fried pockets of dough filled with tomato and mozzarella.

● Visit local markets in Bari and Lecce for fresh goods, or take a cooking lesson to learn how to prepare traditional Puglian foods.

Explore the Olive Groves.

Puglia is recognized as the "olive oil capital" of Italy, with enormous fields of old olive trees stretching as far as the eye can see. Take a tour of an olive farm to learn about the whole process of producing olive oil, from harvest to pressing.

● Visit Masseria San Domenico in Savelletri or Frantoio Ipogeo in Bari for real olive oil tastings. Don't pass up the opportunity to acquire a bottle of Puglian extra virgin olive oil as a keepsake.

Wander through historic towns and villages.

The beauty of Puglia is found not only in its natural beauty but also in its charming cities and villages. Wander around the historic districts, appreciate the typical Trulli homes in Alberobello, or discover Matera's maze-like lanes and old cave dwellings.

● Exploration Tips:

• Explore Lecce's cobblestone streets and see the stunning Baroque buildings.

Visit Polignano a Mare at sunset to enjoy stunning views of the Adriatic Sea.

Immerse yourself in local festivals

Puglia's festivals provide an excellent opportunity to learn about local culture, music, and customs. From the La Notte della Taranta in Salento to the Festa di San Nicola in Bari, there is always a celebration going on.

● Check the festival schedule to plan your vacation around one of these events. You'll see exciting parades, traditional music, dancing, and real regional performances.

Participate in a Wine Tour

Puglia is home to various vineyards that produce exceptional wines, particularly the Primitivo and Negroamaro kinds. A wine tour is a must-do for wine enthusiasts, as it allows you to taste regional wines and learn about the production process.

● Visit Cantine Due Palme or Masseria Li Veli for guided tours and tastings of local wines, followed by a lunch pairing.

Appreciate the Regional Architecture

Puglia's architectural style is just as varied as its scenery. From the ancient Trulli dwellings of Alberobello to the spectacular Romanesque and Baroque cathedrals of Lecce, the architecture reflects the region's rich past.

● Don't miss:

The Castel del Monte, erected by Emperor Frederick II, is a UNESCO World Heritage monument and a must-see attraction.

• The beautiful Basilica di San Nicola in Bari is a pilgrimage monument that highlights Puglia's historical and religious importance.

Explore via bicycle or boat.

Renting a bike or joining a boat excursion is an active way to discover Puglia's breathtaking surroundings. Cycling along the Salento Coast or Gargano National Park is an excellent way to see the region's picturesque landscape and coastline.

Boat Tours: Discover the caverns of Polignano a Mare or the pristine seas of Gargano National Park. Many local providers provide boat trips, which are an excellent opportunity to see the region's shoreline from a new angle.

Don't rush; stay longer.

Consider extending your time in Puglia to fully immerse yourself in the local culture. Puglia is not an area to speed through; it should be enjoyed slowly. Spend a few days in each town, taking time to explore the countryside and soak in the local ambience.

Consider staying at a historic Masseria (country estate) for a true taste of Puglia's rural lifestyle.

Following these guidelines will guarantee that your Puglia vacation is full of adventures and memories. Embrace the slower pace, appreciate the cuisine, and go beyond the tourist destinations to discover the genuine beauty of this mysterious Italian province.

Bonus

Simple Common Phrases to Help You Interact With Locals

Learning a few basic Italian words will greatly improve your stay in Puglia. Using fundamental greetings and expressions allows you to not only respect the local culture but also connect more honestly with the individuals you encounter. Italians admire guests who attempt to speak their language, even if it is just a few words. This supplementary portion of the book contains easy, important words that can help you negotiate everyday encounters, such as ordering meals, asking for directions, or engaging in informal discussions. Mastering these words will make your Puglia experience more pleasurable and memorable since you will feel more integrated into the local way of life.

Useful phrase.

Greetings and Polite Expressions

● Ciao (Hello/Hi)

● Greetings – Good morning.

● Good evening, buonasera.

● Arrivederci – Goodbye

● Per favore: Please

● Grazie (Thank you)

● Prego, you are welcome.

● Excuse me.

● Sorry, where are you? – Excuse me; where is…?

Getting Around

● Where is the station located? – Where is the station?

● How much does it cost? How much does it cost?

● What time does the train depart? – What time is the train leaving?

● Can you help me? – Can you assist me?

● Is there an autobus for…? Is there a bus to…?

Dining & Food

I would like a table for two, please.

● The menu, please.

● What is your advice? – What would you recommend?

● Can I access my account? – Can I get the bill?

- It is delightful! – It is excellent!

Shopping

- How much does this cost? – How much is this?

- Can I pay with a credit card? – Can I pay with a credit card?

- Can you give me a bag? Can you offer me a bag?

- I am just looking.

Directions

- Where is...? – Where's...?

- A destra / a sinistra: Right / Left

- Is it far from here? – Is it far from here?

- Proceed straight ahead.

Emergency Situations

- Need assistance! – Help!

- Book an ambulance! – Call an ambulance!

- Where is the hospital? – Where's the hospital?

- I need a doctor.

General Questions

- Would you want to stay? – How are you doing?

- Hello, my name is [Your Name].

- Do you speak English? – Can you speak English?

- I do not speak Italian very well.

- Can I speak in English? – Can I speak English?

Travel Journal

Date	Destination /Stop	Key Activities/Excursions	Memorable Moments	Food Tried/Restaurants	Thoughts & Reflections	Photos Taken (Yes/No)
Day 1						
Day 2						
Day 3						
Day 4						
Day 5						
Day 6						
Day 7						
Packing List:		Special Memories to Remember:			Important Contacts/Information	

Useful website.

General Travel Information:
● Puglia Tourism Official Website.
Website address: www.viaggiareinpuglia.it.
This official tourist web gives thorough information on Puglia's attractions, activities, and lodgings.

● Visit Italy., the official tourism website.
Website: www.italia.it/en.
Provides extensive travel guides for Italy, including Puglia, with recommendations on sights to visit, cuisine, culture, and activities.

Transportation:
● Trenitalia: Italian Railways
Website address: www.trenitalia.com.
Contact: 892021 (from Italy) or +39 06 68475475 (international).
Book rail tickets and check timetables across Italy, including regional connections in Puglia.

● Italo Treno (High-speed trains)
Website: www.italotreno.it.
Contact: 060708 (from Italy) or +39 06 435 48 481 (international).
For scheduling high-speed trains between major Italian cities, including Bari.

● Autolinee Pugliese (Puglia Bus Service)
Website address: www.autolineepugliese.it
Contact: +39 080 552 0633.
For bus routes and timetables in Puglia, including long-distance and local.

● Puglia Car Rental
Website: www.puglia-rent.com.
Contact: +39 080 527 2010.
Provides automobile rentals for touring Puglia's rural and coastal districts.

Airports:
- Bari Karol Wojtyła Airport.
Website: www.aeroportidipuglia.it/en/bari.
Contact: +39 080 580 0200.
The principal airport in Puglia, with flights to important European and worldwide destinations.

● Brindisi Salento Airport.
Website address: www.aeroportobrindisi.com.
Contact: +39 0831 419711.
Provides local and international flights to Brindisi and the neighbouring regions.

Tourist Information Centers:
● Bari Tourist Office.
Address: Piazza del Ferrarese 70122 Bari.
Contact: +39 080 522 9098.
Website: www.bari.it/turismo.
Located in the city centre, it provides brochures and local information.

● Lecce Tourist Office.
Address: Piazza Sant'Oronzo, 73100 Lecce
Contact: +39 0832 246517.
Website address: www.comune.lecce.it.
A fantastic resource for travellers visiting the Baroque city of Lecce.

● Polignano a Mare Tourist Office.
Address: Via Risorgimento, 70044 Polignano a Mare.
Contact: +39 080 424 0222.
Offers tourist information such as maps, events, and area excursions.

Emergency services:
● Emergency numbers (police, ambulance, fire)
Contact 112 (the EU-wide emergency hotline).

● Local Medical Assistance (Health Services).
Contact: +39 0831 550 555 (Lecce Medical Centre).
For emergency medical services, including hospitals and clinics across Puglia.

Useful Apps:
● Trenitalia App – Book and check train timetables in Italy.
● Italo Treno App: Book high-speed train tickets and track timetables.
● The Moovit app provides public transportation routes and timetables for cities throughout Puglia.

A heartfelt request for review and feedback.

Dear Readers,

Thank you for selecting this book to accompany you on your vacation across the beautiful area of Puglia. Writing this book has been a labour of love and commitment, taking me deep into the heart of this magnificent country. From its old stone alleyways to its sun-kissed shores, every aspect of this book was designed to ensure that you not only visit but also actually experience Puglia.

As a travel guide writer, my goal has always been to give you not just accurate and useful information, but also the type of insights that will make your trip memorable. This book comprises months of painstaking study, numerous hours spent exploring Puglia, and major time and resource investments—travelling across villages, sampling local delicacies, and learning from the people who live here. Every chapter was created to help you discover the charm of Puglia, just like I did.

Your favourable evaluation and opinions are not only very helpful to me as an author, but also critical to my development as a travel guide writer. Your remarks help me continue my adventure, allowing me to develop and provide you with even more fascinating information. Each review you give reflects how effectively this guide benefitted you, and it has a direct influence on my capacity to continue providing high-quality, well-researched recommendations.

If this book has helped you plan your journey or motivated you to discover Puglia's hidden jewels, I would appreciate it if you could write a review. Your ideas not only inspire me to keep writing, but they also give future readers the confidence to go on their travels in Puglia.

Thank you for your trust, time, and support. I hope you enjoyed reading this tutorial as much as I enjoyed writing it. Your input matters more than words can say, and it will serve as a guidepost in my continuous attempts to share the world's beauties with those who seek them.

With genuine appreciation,

Carole J. Harvey

Made in United States
Troutdale, OR
01/11/2025